BEING A
BRILLIANT THINKER

Gayatri Kalra Sehgal is an accomplished artist. Educating young children, with an engaging dash of creativity, was a new dream for her. She has attended seminars, intensive workshops and exclusive courses on child development, curriculum design, effective communication, train the trainer, etc., helping her understand the specific requirements of children.

She has set up a Day Care Centre and two schools, first as the principal and later as a dean, and carefully designed the academic curricula in both roles. She has innovated and revolutionized the novel way of writing report cards called 'Child's Intelligence Profile'.

Presently, she conducts seminars for distinguished educators and creates awareness among parents of differently abled children. This workbook is an extensive collection of her experiences and vision to create global leaders for tomorrow. She has also authored *Winning Strategies for Parents SUPER CHILD! Unlocking the Secrets of Working Memory, Being a Mathematician: Mastering Secrets of Mental Math* and *Being a Creative Genius: Mastering Activities That Inspire Creativity.*

SKILLS THAT BUILD

BEING A
BRILLIANT THINKER

Mastering Intelligent Thinking Skills

Gayatri Kalra Sehgal

Published by
Rupa Publications India Pvt. Ltd 2019
7/16, Ansari Road, Daryaganj
New Delhi 110002

Sales Centres:

Allahabad Bengaluru Chennai
Hyderabad Jaipur Kathmandu
Kolkata Mumbai

Copyright © Gayatri Kalra Sehgal 2019

While every effort has been made to verify the authenticity of the information contained in this book, the publisher and the author are in no way liable for the use of the information contained in this book.

All rights reserved.
No part of this publication may be reproduced, transmitted, or stored in a retrieval system, in any form or by any means, electronic, mechanical, photocopying, recording or otherwise, without the prior permission of the publisher.

ISBN: 978-93-5333-484-0

First impression 2019

10 9 8 7 6 5 4 3 2 1

The moral right of the author has been asserted.

Printed by HT Media Ltd, Gr. Noida

This book is sold subject to the condition that it shall not, by way of trade or otherwise, be lent, resold, hired out, or otherwise circulated, without the publisher's prior consent, in any form of binding or cover other than that in which it is published.

To my sons,

Divyamshu and Kuber

Contents

Foreword | *xiii*

Introduction | 1
How to Use the Book in the Best Way | 17

MEMORY AND ASSOCIATION

Activity 1: The Famous Uncle! | 25
Activity 2: Fire Drill! | 27
Activity 3: Screaming at the Cinema! | 29
Activity 4: Graffiti, Graffiti on the Wall! | 31
Activity 5: History of a Toothbrush! | 33
Activity 6: In Conversation with the Mr Cupboard! | 36
Activity 7: Pillow, Pillow on the Bed, Tell Me the Truth in His or Her Head! | 38
Activity 8: Crime Petrol! | 40
Activity 9: Record the Changes! | 42
Activity 10: Technocrats! | 44
Activity 11: The Time Machine! | 47
Activity 12: Junkyard Sculptors! | 49

SYNTHESIZE AND REFORMULATE

Activity 13: Zero Gravity on Earth! | 53
Activity 14: Flying Apples! | 55
Activity 15: Yapping Utensils and the Smart Bin! | 57

Activity 16: The Shower in the Bathroom! | 59
Activity 17: Device for My Trek to the Jungle! | 62
Activity 18: Hi-Tech Shoes! | 64
Activity 19: Surprise Trip to the Space! | 66
Activity 20: Wounded Animal on the Road! | 69
Activity 21: Food for All! | 72

APPLY AND TEST
Activity 22: Cheater Cock! | 77
Activity 23: Dino in the Town! | 79
Activity 24: Zero Pollution Day! | 82
Activity 25: Environment Summit! | 84
Activity 26: Road Safety Rules! | 86
Activity 27: Bus Safety Rules! | 89
Activity 28: Personal Safety Rules! | 92
Activity 29: Stuck in the Lift! | 95
Activity 30: Fire Safety! | 97
Activity 31: Watch in the Aquarium! | 99
Activity 32: Blind Person Crossing the Road! | 101

ANALYZE AND EVALUATE
Activity 33: A Visit to an Old-age Home! | 105
Activity 34: Lost during a Jungle Safari! | 107
Activity 35: Lost in the Jungle! | 109
Activity 36: Lost in the Ocean! | 111
Activity 37: Peels in the Park! | 113
Activity 38: Pass to the Chocolate Factory! | 115
Activity 39: Fly with the Gas Balloons! | 117

Activity 40: Cousin's Wedding! | 119
Activity 41: Meeting a Mermaid! | 121
Activity 42: Visit to a Construction Site–I! | 123
Activity 42: Visit to a Construction Site–II! | 125

EVIDENCE AND INFERENCE
Activity 43: Chocolate Rain! | 129
Activity 44: Mighty Wings to Fly! | 131
Activity 45: Granddad's Birthday! | 134
Activity 46: Tinkle in the Toilet! | 136
Activity 47: Trip in the Hot-Air-Balloon! | 138
Activity 48: Visit to the Doctor! | 140
Activity 49: Mother's Day Party! | 142
Activity 50: Pet in the Rocket! | 144
Activity 51: Diwali *Ke Mithai*! | 146
Activity 52: Santa's Secret Gift! | 148
Activity 53: Pyjama Party! | 150
Activity 54: The Lost House Key! | 152
Activity 55: Flying Driverless Car! | 154

UNDERSTANDING AND PROBLEM-SOLVING
Activity 56: Fall before the Finish Line! | 159
Activity 57: Visit to the Museum! | 161
Activity 58: No Electricity! | 163
Activity 59: Meeting a Butterfly Fairy! | 165
Activity 60: Tell a Fairy Tale Day! | 167
Activity 61: A Giant Robot Friend! | 169
Activity 62: A Milkshake with Superman! | 171

Activity 63: Suitcase on the Road! | 173
Activity 64: When Sam Ran Away! | 175
Activity 65: Feeding the Animals! | 177
Activity 66: The Mango Tree! | 179
Activity 67: Thirsty Summer! | 181
Activity 68: Terry's Medicine! | 183
Activity 69: One Stormy Evening…! | 185
Activity 70: The Treasure Chest! | 187
Activity 71: Grandpa's Radio! | 189
Activity 72: Crown in the Garden! | 191
Activity 73: Invisible Me! | 193
Activity 74: The Security Guard! | 196
Activity 75: The Secret Door! | 198

Conclusion | 201
Acknowledgements | 203

*Thinking is dynamic.
It is a continuous process to achieve
freedom and strength of knowledge
by perfecting the power of Self.*

Foreword

When I read *Being a Brilliant Thinker: Mastering Intelligent Thinking Skills* by Gayatri Kalra Sehgal with the intention of just browsing like I do with many other books, I was surprised that I couldn't put it down for even a minute. I had finished reading the book in just one sitting. The reason being that Gayatri is an accomplished artist with a lot of creativity and intrinsic knowledge of putting things across—the main message being 'intelligent thinking can be developed and nurtured in students'. It is unfortunate that intelligent thinking is, at present, rarely taught in schools.

Thinking is a mental process in which the students form psychological associations and models of their tiny world. Intelligent thinking, in fact, is manipulating information when we form concepts, engage in problem-solving, reason and make fruitful decisions. Most of the times, a problem remains to be a problem because of lack of intelligent thinking. This promotes the 'Problem Based Learning' concept.

Gayatri, in her book, has explained the basic features of thinking, ways to enhance capabilities of thinking amongst children, methods to gauge the result of the thinking process, and techniques by which the thinking process leads the child to face the ever-expanding universe of knowledge.

This is a must-read book for all the educators, teachers and parents.

Anshul B. Sharma
Chairman, Shastri Group of Institutes

Dear Reader,

If you are in a time machine and get transported twenty years into the future, what skills would you require to add to your CV? List them here:

Read on!

Introduction

Researchers today believe that 65 per cent of the student population will be employed in challenging jobs. However, the bigger challenge is that futuristic jobs don't exist yet. A seven-year-old child, today, will become an active professional in the next sixteen to seventeen years and will continue to work until the next thirty-five to forty years of his or her life. During the considerable time that an individual is employed, there will be drastic changes in the job market and only individuals who have developed next-generation skills will be able to adapt rapidly and thrive in a dynamic job market. Many necessary skills considered valuable a decade ago are now obsolete, and there is no doubt that several skills that we possess today will become obsolete in future.

Technology will progressively replace talented people. Many jobs that are available to people today will be automated in the not too distant future, and only those with irreplaceable skills will survive in such situations. Intelligent machines will perform better than any 'rule-based' job. Those, which are 'not' rule-based, will provide people opportunities to excel. To prepare the human capital to excel in this near future, they must be adequately equipped with the most relevant skills.

While necessary qualifications and knowledge are important, students today require opportunities to become creative individuals with a critical mind. The qualities of a creative individual will help him or her to deal with the challenges in a professional space.

Schools today are great at teaching the basic skills, which are the three Rs—reading, writing and arithmetic. However, most schools do not have the necessary expertise and the effective capacity to teach futuristic skills in the right manner. Let us consider a situation, where a teacher is concerned about a 7-years-old's handwriting, as it is not at par with the other students of the same age. The question here is—if the other skills of the child are well developed, are handwriting skills really an overriding concern? Are we being reasonable in our approach towards the child for being unable to write well? Scratch the polished surface and look at the fundamental problem. If we allow the child to type on the keyboard, it will adequately equip the child to be future ready. Ask yourself—when was the last time you scribbled 200 words with a pen? Now, rethink keeping in mind the future generations. How do you think the present generation is going to use a pen or a pencil to write as a habit? However, if the child is uninterested in writing using a pen or a pencil, is it the only medium of writing for the future generations?

Handwriting is only a skill. If the child is unable to cope, first try to identify the problem. Despite the alternative, if the child is unable to cope, offer support to him or her of another kind; for example, give the child a keyboard to type. Problem solved!

Once we have the solution to the problem, it becomes a way of life. So, what are the necessary skills required by future generations?

The curricula should offer the core purpose of education. It should prepare the future generations with effective education, empower and equip them to be productive and successful individuals. It is undoubtedly a futuristic approach towards deeper learning.

As parents, we need to change our method of explaining ways to deal with a problem to the child, which will enable him or her to think in a particular manner. This will encourage them to ask questions.

Children, today, need to be provided with a vast assortment of learning resources that stimulate their thinking towards problem-solving techniques and generate useful solutions.

The structured curriculum needs to be redirected and refocussed towards the 'whys' and 'hows' of everything. The revised curriculum will radically transform the pattern of learning by incorporating ways to acquire skills required for the upcoming generations. Offering students a viable option to enhance their process of thinking progressively to form and express opinions will help them become creative and have critical minds.

Let's begin by discussing the different types of 'thinking':

1. Concrete Thinking
2. Abstract Thinking
3. Convergent Thinking
4. Divergent Thinking
5. Creative Thinking
6. Analytical Thinking
7. Sequential (linear) Thinking
8. Critical Thinking

Let us understand each type of thinking.

1. *Concrete Thinking*:
   It focusses on factual events and physical objects. It is one dimensional and literal.

2. *Abstract Thinking*:
   Abstract thinking is about ideas and concepts, such as justice or love rather than actual concrete experiences. Abstract thinkers think about *why* things are the way they are. They connect *how* they feel to *what* they think.

3. *Convergent Thinking*:
   It is a process of creating logical steps to determine the single best solution for a particular problem. It relies more on logic and less on the creative approach to solving a problem. It works best in situations, where a single correct answer is possible and the solution can be discovered by analysing the stored information. In other words, it means dealing with numerous facts to find only one precise answer. Many thoughts, including knowledge, decision and evaluation converge into one accurate answer.

4. *Divergent Thinking*:
   It is the opposite of convergent thinking. It is a thought process or a method used to generate multiple creative ideas by exploring as many possible situations to generate novel solutions to the problem. It occurs in a free-flowing, spontaneous and non-linear manner, such that the ideas are generated in an emergent cognitive fashion. After the process of divergent thinking is complete, ideas and information are organized and structured.

5. *Creative Thinking*:
   It is a creative process, involving fertile imagination, invention, changing, designing and creation. It progressively develops unorthodox solutions that do not depend wholly on past or current solutions. Creative thinking is focussed naturally on unlimited possibilities. It encourages you to see things differently and deal in a better way with uncertainties.

6. *Critical Thinking*:
   Critical thinking diligently seeks to accurately access the comparative worth or content validity of something that exists at present. It is convergent and is focussed on

reasonable probability. It is a cognitive process that sufficiently involves analysis, breaking down, comparing, sequencing and evaluating information.

7. *Analytical Thinking*:
Analytical thinking involves visual thinking that contributes meaningfully to the unique ability to solve potential problems quickly and effectively. It involves a methodical approach to the thought process, allowing one to break down complex problems into distinct and manageable components. It is the ability to collect, visualize and analyse information in detail to see a problem or a situation from diverse point of views. Analytical skills allow you to remedy complex problems by making decisions in the most effective way.

8. *Sequential (linear) Thinking*:
Sequential, or linear, thinking is the intellectual ability to process and organize information in a 'systematic' way. Sequential thinking is carefully executed in a developed series of logical steps to arrive at a logical conclusion or correctly solve a problem. It is similar to designing a specific program for a compatible computer, i.e., typically following a step-by-step process of properly executing a specific task.

As you can see, there are many types of thinking processes. However, a lot of importance has been given to critical and then to analytical thinking.

So, should a parent focus only on typically developing critical thinking or analytical thinking? Are the other types of thinking unnecessary or obsolete?

Hold on!

My fundamental question undoubtedly remains: what is 'thinking'?

Researchers have been able to trace the electric tracks of thinking in the brain, but that does not translate into real knowledge of what it really is and what people do when they say they are 'thinking'. Thinking is a creative process and a subjective experience. There is enough evidence for humans to be at the top of the animal kingdom because of our superior intelligence, mental powers and abilities to reason and think.

'Thinking' represents a creative chain of processes. It associates the previously acquired information with the new information to synthesize, reformulate, apply, test, analyse and evaluate to draw inferences to efficiently generate practical and creative solutions, with established evidence to understand and solve a problem by translating the totality of experiences about a topic on an imaginary screen inside the brain.

Let us understand the rocket science behind 'thinking' with a simple example—the 'Thinking Wheel'.
Let us understand the six links of the 'Thinking Wheel'.

'Thinking' can be developed by mental effort, intellectual consistency and focussed practice, and hence, it becomes a necessary 'skill' for everybody. It is not restricted to age, race or socioe-conomic status. 'Thinking' can be developed provided the structure of the process is followed carefully. It is a creative chain of processes, and the links between each circle represent the path to develop thinking. When we develop the chain of the processes in thinking, all the other types of thinking are enhanced. We are able to offer a child the opportunity to be a 'holistic-thinker', which is the primary skill required to make the child future-ready.

Let us understand what the processes are and why it is important to link each process.

Introduction

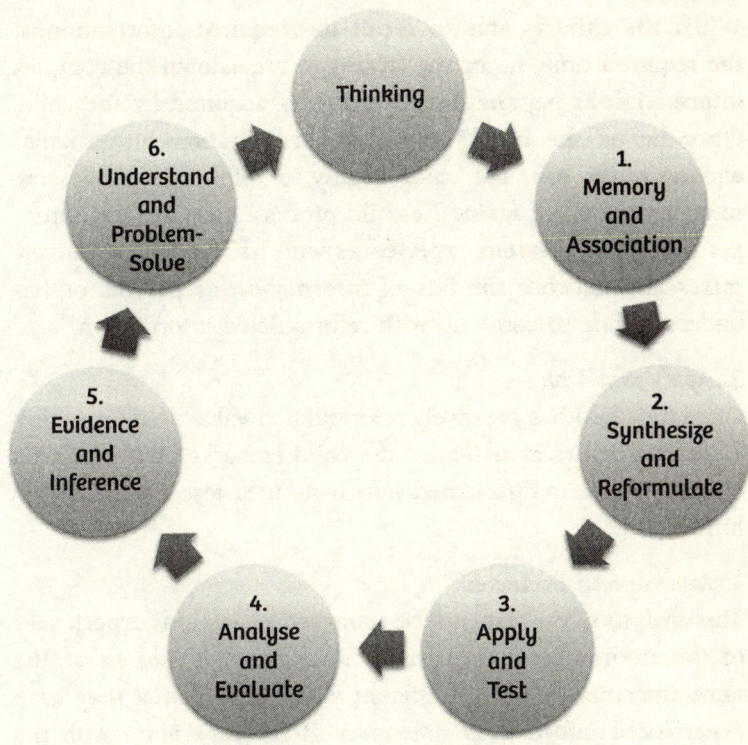

1. *Memory and Association*:

Children are born with information programmed into their memory. As the child experiences and receives more information from the surroundings, he or she begins to associate this newly acquired information with the already present information in the brain. As the information is repeated often, the child begins to build a reservoir of 'associations', which gets stored in the nerve pathways in the brain as a memory to be recalled when required.

2. *Synthesize and Reformulate*:
When the child is able to recall the required information at the required time, he or she begins to breakdown the complex information as per the mental maturity acquired by the child. Once he or she breaks down the information into smaller and narrower bits, the child begins to reformulate the same information. Once again, the child processes the information as per his or her previous experiences with it. The child creatively mixes and matches the bits of information as per his or her understanding to come up with reformulated information.

3. *Apply and Test*:
Once the child has creatively reformulated valuable information as per his or her experiences, the child embarks on the process of applying the reformulated information to test if it works for him or her.

4. *Analyse and Evaluate*:
This analysis of the tests will be subjected to previous experiences of the information. The reason why everybody looks at the same information with a different perspective is that they have experienced information differently. If the experience with the information was 'good' for the child, the subsequent evaluation of information would be positive; if the experience with information was 'bad', the subsequent information evaluated would be negative. Let us suppose that every time the child does his or her home assignments well, the child gets lots of appreciation from the parents. On the other hand, each time the child refuses to eat vegetables, he or she observes parents get concerned or upset. Hence, the child begins to analyse the experiences and evaluates his or her experiences based on previous experiences.

Similarly, in the process of thinking, the child begins to experiment and test his or her analysis. For example, if the child wishes to seek your attention and throws a tantrum, and you react to it each time; the child tests your reaction to the same situation the next time. If the parent invariably gives in to the demands of the child, he or she begins develop a habit. Next time, when the parent is firm about 'not' giving in to the child's relentless demands, the child throws a more stressful tantrum to test you. The idea is to remain firm from the beginning so that each time the child tests the limits, he or she gets a consistent reply, and the child gets the message more and more clearly.

5. *Evidence and Inference:*
When you react to the situation, each time the child does so, the child tests your reaction to the same situation. When the child has analysed and tested the results of a situation, he or she begins to establish the evidence with relevant information/data/statistics to draw the inference for a given situation. In the above-mentioned example, the child evaluates your response to establish evidence by testing you repeatedly to draw the inference to behave in a particular manner.

6. *Understand and Problem-solving*:
The inferences help the child understand and resolve the problem at hand. However, we need to understand the parallels between mental maturity and growth.

Mental maturity provides a state of readiness for the child to understand. However, the sense organs that are used to naturally absorb valuable information and perceive knowledge must be functionally mature to develop understanding. This positively enhances the information-processing abilities essential to understand complex problems, situations and reasoning in a child.

Although the maturation is known to have a predictable pattern, these patterns are unique for each child.

Understanding a situation or a topic helps the child to develop concepts. The development of concepts indicates what a child 'knows', 'recognizes' and 'believes', and as a result, how he or she will react to a situation. The more the accuracy a child has about the concept, the greater is the understanding in him or her.

As compared to adults, children have limited knowledge as they have experienced limited information. Hence, the development of concepts becomes a difficult process in children. However, concepts become clear as the child's ability to associate information increases.

Rather than developing thinking only in one dimension, the above-mentioned six steps in the 'thinking wheel' helps the child develop thinking effectively in any sphere of life. The 'holistic thinker' will be empowered to think in multiple dimensions to create novel solutions to a given task.

Now that we have understood what is 'thinking', let us understand the factors that can hamper its rate of development.

Factors Affecting Thinking:

1. *Restrictions to Disagree*:
When too many restrictions are laid on children and they are not allowed to be non-conforming, or to disagree with what is being said or done, parents or facilitators restrict the process of thinking of the child to form their own opinions.

2. *Discipline with Discounts*:
When the child is asked to complete a task, such as finishing a glass of milk, and the parent allows the child to waste a quarter glass of milk as and when the child chooses to, the parent agrees to relax the limits of discipline because they are occupied with other things. It gives the child the idea to pick on discounts when they wish to.

3. *Terror of Taking Risks*:
When the insecurity in parents is communicated knowingly or unknowingly to children, they terrorize the child and limit his or her capability to take risks.

4. *The Hearty Harsh Comments*:
Many times, adults (I will not say UNKNOWINGLY) smirk, pass harsh comments, snide remarks at the child's small advancements made towards learning. The child instantly withdraws from thinking.

5. *Superb Student Scores*:
Scores on the report cards have done more damage to the personality of the child than doing any good to reflect the true development of learning. Moreover, the education system does not provide any assessment about the development of thinking in the process of learning. We need to appreciate improvement rather than the superfluous scores achieved by the child.

Factors Responsible to Promote Thinking:

1. *Multi-Sensorial Learning*:
We all use our sense organs to absorb information. Everybody uses one preferred sense organ to absorb maximum information than the other. A rich assortment of open-ended materials encourages the children to absorb information using different sense organs. It expands their thinking. A learner should be offered multi-sensorial and hands-on experience for learning such that the capacity to think is enhanced in a child. This approach towards thinking helps the child to blend emotions, visuals, words, concepts, perceptions and intuitions to enhance thinking.

2. Independent and Interdependent Learning:
Ensure that the child works in different work environments where he or she gets the opportunity to work without the help of adults and works interdependently with their peers. It helps the child perceive information with a different and deeper dimension.

3. Read with the Children:
Parents who read with their children and ask open-ended questions during the reading sessions motivate the child to think in different situations. Reading with the children helps them think and develop concepts.

4. Active Listening:
Hearing and listening (to the children) have different meanings. Hearing is a sense that helps one receive sound waves and noise through our ears. However, listening is receiving sound waves, and the listener pays full attention to understand the feelings expressed by words and sentences spoken. Similarly, when the child is talking to the parents or the facilitator, and if they are busy over the phone, adults are only 'hearing' the child and not 'listening' to what he or she is saying. Keep all your gadgets away and participate in the conversation with your child. It is only then, that the communication loop is completed, and the child gets more opportunities to think. If the child is asking questions, it means that he or she is curious to know the answers.

Feed the child's curiosity by having open-ended conversations.

5. Appreciate Improvement:
Each child has a learning pace, and we not only need to appreciate it but also respect it genuinely. Every little effort by the child needs to be appreciated such that the child gets positively motivated towards thinking and learning openly. *Remember to compare the*

child with his or her own capabilities rather than in comparison with other children.

'Hyper-Me-*Safetya*'!

At this juncture, I would like to introduce you to a different tangent of thinking. I call it Hyper-Me-*Safetya*! No, this funny term is not a term written anywhere online or even in those big, fat dictionaries, but it has to be dealt seriously.

In simple words:
Hyper: Unusual energy (to think)
Me: Myself
Safetya: Safety
It means: Unusual energy to think about my own safety!

In the present world of social media, where the safety and security of a person is at stake, we unknowingly expose our children to a lot of danger in the surrounding. Research has proven that there is a marked increase in child abuse. Hence, it becomes imperative for parents to help the children be aware and think critically about any situation or a person to avoid any foreseeable danger—Hyper-Me-*Safetya*! We have to enable the children to be capable of *thinking about their safety!*

Now, the question arises as to how do we do this. Obviously, we cannot scare the child about every person walking on the road; however, there are three key issues we have to ensure that the child is capable of understanding, assessing and taking decisions prudently to get out of any unwanted dangerous situation:

1. How do we make the child aware of the potential dangers in the environment?
2. How does the child assess if the person whom they are calling out for help is a good or a bad person?
3. If the child is in a 'situation', we have to ensure that he

or she does not get scared and lose confidence to fight the situation, but the child needs to ensure his or her own safety.

How do we help the child think so that he or she is able to assess the danger? For sure, we cannot keep nagging about safety and security every day.

Going forward, in this stand-alone segment of 'Hyper-Me-Safetya', I shall give you a set of questions to tickle your child's thought processes in a particular situation while learning a topic or playing a game. Bring these questions into your daily conversations such that the thinking pattern serves as a root for nurturing a sapling to grow into a strong plant!

Remember that the key to evaluate the information relating to human development is to maintain a healthy dose of scepticism. No source of information is accurate forever.

Some hypothetical situations are given to understand the questions. However, you will need to tweak the questions to suit your requirements:

Situation 1:

The child is watching his or her favourite television programme.

Ask the child if the advice given by the 'hero' to the 'villain' in the show is justified in real life. Are all the advice on the television or in print media equally valid and accurate? Can you write down the guidelines or recommendations that you think are reasonable?

Situation 2:

A friend in the class tells your child that the next day is not a holiday.

Is the friend a genuine source of information? If not, then

find out if he or she is a reliable source of information. Ask your child to enquire about the information from his or her teacher. Encourage him or her to evaluate the credentials of their friend who had provided the information.

Situation 3:

Your child's friends say that they play throughout the year, study for seven days before the exams, and get good scores.

Ask your child if he or she thinks that the information is believable.

Is the statement based on transparency? What were the methods of studying during the year the friend had adopted? Did the friend study late at night while others were asleep? What do the results reveal?

Think about the ways the findings were obtained before accepting them?

Situation 4:

The new friend in the society who has recently shifted is ill mannered.

Do not assume it to be true just because many people believe in something. Investigate. Meet the friend personally. If what you find is not true, provide and establish enough evidence about your new friend.

Situation 5:

Clipping nails on the bed is a bad omen.

Encourage the child to consider the cultural context of the information. Is the assertion valid in any context? Does the statement hold true in all the cultures?

Scientific evaluations have often provided enough evidence

that some of the most basic presumptions about the effectiveness of various beliefs are invalid. However, could there be any rational arguments behind the statement you can come up with?

During the daily conversations, ask such questions to your child and allow them the time to think and come up with their answers. Remember, sometimes children take days to think about a topic and then come up with their solutions. However, if we keep asking relevant questions and turn it into a habit, the thinking process will gradually be trained and the child will be able to come up with the answers faster. Remember not to be in a hurry. Your target is to get them to think clearly, while maintaining your focus.

NOTE: Keep in mind that this book is intended to provide ideas for beginners on safety rules to teach young children. By educating children in their primary years, they will know how to protect themselves in different situations while growing up. For optimal safety, I recommend reviewing to gain further knowledge about children's safety.

How to Use the Book in the Best Way

Each activity, or a situation, given in the book has specific goals to be achieved. These goals are specific to the process of thinking that needs to be focussed on. Each Activity, or engagement, is designed with five to six significant segments. Let us adequately understand each unique segment.

1. Getting Ready:

It tells the reader how to prepare the children for the activity. It is always better to prepare beforehand, as children begin to work proactively and you would not want to lose a moment of spontaneity.

2. Resources Required:

Most of the Resources Required for the activities are available at your homes. They need not be bought from stores. However, the most crucial part of the resources is the quality time parents and facilitators spend with their children. It will undoubtedly help you take the child away from the screen and bond with nature, family and friends. Naturally, having healthy, warm and funny conversations will be an inevitable way to encouraging the child to develop the desired skills. Most of the activities and engagements are not timed, as the children may require more time than allotted to come up with ideas. However, you may time the activities for a more active engagement.

3. Proposed Situation:

After the children have all the Resources Required for the activity, this step will help parents create a situation for their children. It will serve as a conversation starter for parents and facilitators. Parents can develop this segment as per their requirement. However, they must remember that as they alter the situation according to their requirements, 'Resources Required' and 'Getting Ready' would also change. Therefore, prepare accordingly.

4. Tickle the Thoughts:

Once the idea has been proposed to the child, allow him to understand the open-ended questions and ensure to maintain the element of fun throughout the activities. 'Tickle the Thoughts' is a set of pointers for parents to facilitate the thinking of the child into the desired direction, without pressurizing the child. Parents may brainstorm and ask as many questions as they wish, ensuring that they do not restrict the child's imagination by giving the answers away too quickly.

*No questions asked **by the** child **is 'right or wrong'**, it is for you to feed the curiosity of the child.*

Give accurate and clear answers to them. If you do not recall the answer to the question, inform the child about it. Team up with the child and search for the answers together.

Allow the child to be non-conforming; it will encourage them to make informed and critically-thought-of opinions!

Your involvement will have a significant impact on the child's development, as you will enable him or her to face complex situations in real life, deal with them practically and think creatively.

While asking questions, we must encourage the children to take risks even when they are wrong, challenge their ideas and reflect on their tasks. We will need to remember that if the child has learned hundreds of facts but hasn't developed the ability to explore possibilities, most of the acquired knowledge is wasted.

5. Goals Achieved:

It is a crucial tool for recognizing the level of thinking the child has achieved during the activity. Remember that thinking is not a static condition, it is a dynamic process, and a child is encouraged to think and conclude in a variety of creative ways.

During the activity, or the engagement, the development and achievement of the child will take you by surprise. *Aim for intellectual diversity.*

Assessment of Improvement:

Assessments are the most crucial areas, where parents and facilitators will need to inspect carefully. Do not judge your child negatively or be biased. The next step is to assess if the child's thinking is improving, or should you propose more situations that will help him or her to achieve the goal.

Since thinking happens in the mind and its result is mostly in the form of actions, how can one assess what the child has typically acquired in terms of learning a specific skill? Has the child's thinking been fostered correctly? Mentioned below are the possible indications that the child will show if their thinking has improved.

1. *Divergent Perspectives:*

The child thinks of as many possible approaches and ideas in engaging in the activity, and is later able to utilize the relevant information in a real-life situation. During your daily conversations, the child will communicate and ask questions from what he or she has learned from the activities.

2. Flexibility of Thoughts:

When you propose different situations to the child, he or she is able to look at it from different perspectives. The child begins to explore, classify, categorize and reformulate other possibilities to come up with novel solutions when exposed to a situation in real life.

3. Increased Level of Curiosity:

You will see that the child has begun to ask you more relevant and irrelevant questions; his or her mind has an unquenchable thirst for information and attempts to come up with more solutions to a given situation.

4. Complexity of Questions:

The child will begin to ask questions in an increasing level of complexity. However, the level of thinking of the child will increase in a graph that is unique for him or her. It will also depend on various factors such as the development and maturity of communication skills to express their thoughts.

5. Taking Risks:

You will observe that the child has begun taking risks to guess the answers correctly, defend their innovative ideas without the fear of being mocked at by their peers. The cognitive ability to take risks will also vary based on the child's level of self-confidence and self-esteem.

6. Imagination and Creativity:

Imaginative and creative children can picture and instinctively create what they haven't already thought of. They have the ability to imagine themselves in different times and places. You will begin

How to Use the Book in the Best Way

to hear the children talk excessively about their imaginations with you. However, it will be subjected to their level of communication skills. If the communication skills are well developed, they will be more expressive. However, if the communication skills are still developing, you will see children making extra efforts to communicate with you, using their facial expressions and body language. When the child's communication skills are still developing, and he or she is excited to express their ideas to you, they might not be able to do so. They might appear frustrated and aggressive. Parents need to be patient to understand the child's newly acquired ways of expression.

Notes: Extra pages have been provided at the end of the book for parents and facilitators to scribble their ideas during a session. Parents may note verbal expressions or stick pictures of the child they are engaged with during an activity to relive the fond memories later.

Activity–1

The Famous Uncle!

RESOURCES REQUIRED
- A paper
- A pen

Getting Ready:
Keep the mood and the surroundings light for 'healthy' and funny conversations!

Proposed Situation:
Hand over papers and pens to the children. Ask them to write down five questions to explain the word 'famous'. Then, they must name their favourite 'famous-in-the-family uncle'. Ask the children to write at least five key questions that they would like to ask 'The Famous Uncle'. Finally, ask them to write down the answers to the questions as well.

Tickle the Thoughts:
1. What does the word 'famous' mean to the children?
2. Ask them how do people become famous?
3. What do the children think 'the famous uncle' is known for?
4. Would they like to role-play or mimic 'the famous uncle?'

Being a Brilliant Thinker

🎯 Goals Achieved
- Better questioning abilities
- Improved visualization
- Ability to understand evidence and inference
- Increased abstract thinking
- Better analytical thinking
- Enhanced critical thinking

Tick-tack Tip

Children enjoy observing funny and peculiar features in familiar people. To add an element of fun to this game, 'the famous uncle' could have a distinct quality of cracking the funniest jokes or making faces. The fundamental idea is to provide the children a setting, where they can have fun and think at the same time!

Activity–2

Fire Drill!

RESOURCES REQUIRED
- A paper
- Colour pencils
- An eraser

Getting Ready:
Hand over papers and colour pencils to the children.

Proposed Situation:
You have had a long day at school, and you decide to sleep early tonight. As you finish brushing your teeth before going to bed, you hear a lot of noise outside your house. You also hear people talking. You go to the window to check what is happening. You see people have gathered at the end of the street and that there is a lot of light there. It does not look like a pleasant scene to you. Suddenly, you hear a loud siren of a fire brigade and you realize that there is a fire in the vicinity. You quickly switch on the television to watch the news. Sadly, many houses were burnt, leaving people homeless and devastated.

Tickle the Thoughts:
1. Ask the children to enact the scene.

Being a Brilliant Thinker

2. How do you know that there is a fire?
3. Have a brainstorming session and ask them to write down questions they would want to ask people who have suffered losses and the bystanders separately.
4. What safety measures should be taken up everybody so that if there is a fire in future, it can be controlled?
5. Ask them to chalk out a plan to provide help to those who have suffered losses.

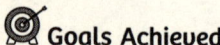
Goals Achieved
- Improved questioning abilities
- Increased reasoning abilities
- Enhanced visualization
- Empathy for people

Tick-tack Tip
The activity will help children to imbibe the feeling of empathy within children for people who are suffering. It will also encourage them to organize help for such people and situations. Accompanying children to the site where a natural disaster has occurred is a persuasive way to encourage them to recognize problems in the real world. It will also make them feel grateful for being safe. However, ensure that you prepare the children for such circumstances.

Activity–3

Screaming at the Cinema!

RESOURCES REQUIRED:
- A paper
- A pencil

Getting Ready:

Ask the children to take their stationery.

Proposed Situation:

You have taken your children to the cinema. Everything is going as planned. The movie is very interesting. During the intermission, you get all the scrumptious food to eat and quickly settle down on your seat to watch the climax of the movie. Suddenly, a man runs out of the cinema, screaming and shouting frantically!

Tickle the Thoughts:

1. Ask the children if they think screaming hysterically at the theatre is a behavioural problem and should be addressed by the authorities. When some fans begin to dance merrily at the theatre, should they be controlled?
2. Ask them what kinds of emergencies can occur at a theatre.
3. Urge them to list the precautionary measures that should be taken in advance to avoid any kind of emergency.

30 Being a Brilliant Thinker

🎯 Goals Achieved
- Improved questioning abilities
- Better reasoning abilities
- Enhanced visualization

Tick-tack Tips
1. As the children ponder over the incident at the theatre, help them understand the proper course of action in case there was an emergency during the movie. Show them the emergency exit from where people can move to a safer place.
2. Share the importance of maintaining mental balance and quick thinking during an emergency.

Activity—4

Graffiti, Graffiti on the Wall!

RESOURCES REQUIRED
- A paper
- A pencil

Getting Ready:

Hand over the resources to the children.

Proposed Situation:

The children are making terrible graffiti in the classroom. The class teacher is very upset with them, as they have soiled the walls of the classroom. She seeks your child's help to come up with solutions to stop this from happening again. In addition, she suggests using a cloth to wipe off the graffiti.

Tickle the Thoughts:

1. Ask the children if all paintings done on walls are called graffiti.
2. Does India have its own type of 'wall-art'?
3. Did artists use the same colour to paint on the walls across the world and why?
4. Ash them if the paintings have a cultural context.

Being a Brilliant Thinker

> **Goals Achieved**
> - Improved questioning abilities
> - Better reasoning abilities
> - Improved visualization

Tick-tack Tips

Share the interesting information with children and ask them if they would like to try wall-art.

1. Graffiti is a creative and expressive form of street art. It includes writings and drawings made on a surface such as a wall or a ceiling. Graffiti dates back to ancient Egypt, ancient Greece and the Roman Empire.
2. In 1967, a high school student from Philadelphia named Darryl McCray, better known for his tagging name 'Cornbread', is the first modern graffiti writer. But it was only in the 1980s that the galleries began to showcase graffiti as an artwork.
3. Warli/Varli is the ancient wall-art form from Maharashtra. It gained its social prominence in the 1970s when Jivya Soma Mashe and his son Balu began painting. The colours used for making Warli are heena, indigo, ochre, black, earthy mud and white. The white colour is made of rice, water and glue. The tribes used a flexible bamboo stick as paintbrushes. These brushes are prepared by beating the bamboo at one end. The paintings were made inside the village huts. They decorated walls with earth, branches and red bricks. The earth gave the wall a red ochre background for the paintings.

Activity–5

History of a Toothbrush!

RESOURCES REQUIRED

- A corrugated sheet
- A pair of child-safe scissors
- A child-safe knife
- A pencil

Getting Ready:
Keep the required stationery ready for every child.

How to Prepare:
1. Ask the children to take corrugated sheet and cut out a large shape of a toothbrush.
2. Ask them to write the history on the handle of the toothbrush. Then, cut strips of corrugated sheets to make the bristles of the brush.
3. Ask them to use the child-safe knife and make incessions on the handle of the toothbrush and fit in these strips.

Proposed Situation:
It is late in the night and your children are planning to go to the washroom before going to bed. They walk towards the washroom, open the bathroom door a little and see a trail of pixie dust

Being a Brilliant Thinker

going up in the sky. They think to themselves, 'Wow, is that some kind of magic!'

Suddenly, they hear the toothbrush talk! The toothbrush tells them that it needs their help!

It needs their help to write about its experiences and turn it into a biography.

Tickle the Thoughts:

1. Ask your children what is a biography and if they have ever read one.
2. Many people believe in magic; ask them if they believe in magic as well.
3. Ask them what they think the toothbrush experiences when it enters a smelly mouth.

Goals Achieved:
- Enhanced abstract thinking
- Improved critical thinking
- Increased associations
- Better reasoning abilities
- Helps to convert imaginative visuals into script

Tick-tack-Tips:
1. Make the best of the fun element and enthusiastically encourage healthy conversations with the children. Encourage them to naturally think using all their senses—eyes to see, nose to smell, etc.

2. Encourage the children not to assume that because many people believe in something, it is necessarily true. Scientific evaluations have often proved that some of the basic presumptions about the effectiveness of various techniques are invalid. In the given situation, 'magic' needs to be put under a crystalline lens.

Activity–6

In Conversation with the Mr Cupboard!

RESOURCES REQUIRED
- A pencil
- A paper to write on
- A mat to sit on

Getting Ready:

Sit comfortably in front of the cupboard with the children.

Proposed Situation:

Urge the children to fix an appointment with Mr Cupboard for an exclusive interview to be published in the local newspaper. Mr Cupboard is very busy hoarding stuff inside.

Tickle the Thoughts:

1. Ask the children how will they approach Mr Cupboard for an appointment.
2. What will they ask Mr Cupboard?
3. Ask them if they think Mr Cupboard likes to be messy.
4. Ask the children how can they help Mr Cupboard.
5. Tell them to write a story to be published in the local newspaper with catchy captions.

Activity-6   37

Goals Achieved
- Enhanced abstract thinking abilities
- Increased creative thinking skills
- Improved analytical thinking
- Better reasoning abilities
- Helps to convert imaginative visuals into script

Tick-tack Tip
Encourage the children to publish the interview with Mr Cupboard in the school's magazine.

Activity–7

Pillow, Pillow on the Bed, Tell Me the Truth in His or Her Head!

RESOURCES REQUIRED

- A bed
- A pillow

Getting Ready:

1. Spare some extra time at night when children go to bed.
2. Every child has his or her secret, such as where they hide their candy away from their sibling, caught being naughty in class, etc. Keep the secrets with you. Play the role of a detective.

Proposed Situation:

Inform the children that their pillow off-late has been informing you some of their top secrets! Give them a hint about one such secret. Tell them to ask the pillow if it did really say so. Ask them to search the pillow for the secrets about their sibling.

(Wait! You will know all their secrets in the next five minutes!)

Tickle the Thoughts:

1. Ask the children if they think the pillow can talk and how did you get to know their secrets.

2. Ask them if they searched the pillow for a microphone.
3. Was the proposed situation based on scientific findings?
4. What were the methods used by you to obtain information about their secrets?

Goals Achieved
- Enhanced abstract thinking
- Improved critical thinking
- Increased analytical thinking
- Better reasoning abilities

Tick-tack Tip

Encourage the children to base their conclusions on research findings. They must cross-examine the methods employed to arrive at any conclusion.

Activity–8

Crime Petrol!

RESOURCES REQUIRED
- A pen
- A paper

Getting Ready:
Have long conversations with your children about community helpers and their responsibilities.

Proposed Situation:
Ask your children about different kinds of crimes in the society. Give them instances of crimes such as theft, animal cruelty, destruction of property, etc. Then, tell them to list these crimes starting from the least serious to the most serious.

Tickle the Thoughts:
1. Ask the children to write at least three reasons why the criminal committed the crime.
2. Was the criminal actually responsible for the crime?
3. What can they do so that the criminal does not commit the crime.

Goals Achieved:
- Improved analytical thinking
- Enhanced critical thinking
- Better investigating abilities
- Increased ability to establish facts

Tick-tack Tips
1. Encourage the children to base their conclusions on the research findings. They must cross-examine the methods used to arrive at any conclusion.
2. Explain to the children that just because people believe in something, it is not necessarily true. Scientific evaluations have often proved that some of the basic assumptions about the effectiveness of various techniques are invalid.

Activity–9

Record the Changes!

RESOURCES REQUIRED
- A pen
- A paper

Getting Ready:

Spare some time to have long conversations with the children about the various changes that they observe in their daily lives. For example, the changes in the weather and seasons. You may share the picture album with your child to show their picture when they were young and compare it to their pictures now.

Proposed Situation:

Ask the children to write at least five things that change rapidly, five things that take a long time to change and five things that change slowly. For example, what melts faster—a glacier or an ice cube from the refrigerator?

Tickle the Thoughts:

1. Ask the children if there is a definite speed of change, which can be used to compare the rate of change.
2. Ask them if they can formulate a standard unit of rate of change.

Activity-9   43

3. What according to them is fast or slow speed?

> 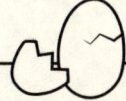 **Goals Achieved**
> - Improved analytical thinking
> - Enhanced critical thinking
> - Better sequential (linear) thinking

Tick-tack Tip

Help the children to understand the difference between anecdotal evidence and scientific evidence. Anecdotal evidence is based on one or two instances of a phenomenon that was encountered haphazardly. However, scientific evidence is based on systematic procedures carried out on a large population.

Activity–10

Technocrats!

RESOURCES REQUIRED
- A pen
- A paper

Getting Ready:

Spare some time to have long conversations with the children. Give them a hand fan and ask them to use it for five minutes. Then, ask them how they can make things easier for themselves.

Proposed Situation:

Ask the children to list all the machines they use during the day. Once they have written down their names, introduce more questions for specific answers such as vending machines, juicers and mixers, ATMs, etc.

Tickle the Thoughts:

1. Ask the children to define machines and how they help us.
2. If your children were to create a machine, ask them what would it look like, and what would be the purpose of that machine? Urge them first to write about the machine and then draw it.
3. Ask them if machines can replace humans altogether.

Activity–10 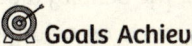 45

4. Can machines learn by themselves? Do the children know about Artificial Intelligence?

> **Goals Achieved**
> - Improved abstract thinking
> - Enhanced divergent thinking
> - Better creative thinking ability

Tick-tack Tips
1. A machine is an apparatus that uses mechanical power. It has several parts. Each part of the machine performs a definite function.
2. Help the children make working model projects. It will help them understand how the machines work, its benefits and the evils linked with it.
3. Artificial intelligence (AI) is the ability of a computer programme or a machine to learn. It is a field of study, which tries to make computers 'intelligent'.
   The uses of AI are:
   - Personalization: Apps use artificial intelligence to enhance your experience. Apps, such as Amazon or Netflix, 'learn' from your previous purchases in order to make suitable recommendations for you. So, the next time you get recommendations from Amazon, know that AI is learning about your preferences from the choices you are making.

- Fraud Detection: Banks use artificial intelligence too. If the bank detects a strange activity in your account, it sends you a quick alert message to determine if the activity was performed by you. Unexpected activity, such as a large amount of financial transactions, could be flagged by the algorithm.
- Social Media: When you receive a notification on Facebook that your account was opened from a different location or a machine, know that AI is doing the job well.
- Email filtering: Email services use artificial intelligence to filter the emails in your inbox. Users can set their spam filters by marking emails as 'spam'.
- Speech or voice recognition: Applications use artificial intelligence to optimize the function of speech recognition. For example, intelligent personal assistants, such as Siri or Alexa.

Activity–11

The Time Machine!

RESOURCES REQUIRED
- 1. A pen
- 2. A paper

Getting Ready:

Spare some time to have long conversations with the children about the past, present and future events. Tell them about stories of their birth, gradually bring the conversation to the present day. Then, ask them what they think will happen the next day, five years later and after ten years.

Proposed Situation:

Imagine that your children are sitting in a time machine that can send them into the future. They sit inside it and turn on the time machine. A pink liquid flows into the tiny key hole. The machine jolts to a start with a loud scary roar and shakes up the entire floor. The lights on it get turned on and they move at the speed of light. Even before they could realise, they have been transported to 2200!

Tickle the Thoughts:

1. What would the time machine look like? Can they draw it?

2. What do they think would be the most amusing experience once they are sent into the future?
3. What will be the most frightening thing?
4. What will take them by surprise?
5. Would they like to live in 2200 or would they want to come back to the present? Why?

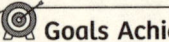

Goals Achieved:
- Improved abstract thinking
- Enhanced divergent thinking
- Better creative thinking

Tick-tack Tips

1. Whatever our creative thinkers imagined an era ago has become a reality today. Allow the children to imagine the unimaginable! Encourage them to think and design a time machine.
2. Give them recyclable material to develop their time machine!

Activity—12

Junkyard Sculptors!

RESOURCES REQUIRED
- A pen
- A paper
- Recyclable material (optional): Old shoeboxes, CDs, pencil boxes, etc.

Getting Ready:
Spare some time to have long and creative conversations with children about the resources available in the environment and how we can recycle them.

Proposed Situation:
Imagine that your children are standing in front of a junkyard that has a variety of recyclable materials that they can use to make amazing things at zero cost. The junkyard has empty shoeboxes, bottles, metal chains, wooden planks, wires, jute ropes, etc.

Tickle the Thoughts:
1. Ask your children to create a list of things they can 'see' at the junkyard.
2. Choose a barren play area. Ask the children to decorate it by using the items in their lists.

3. Ask them if they can draw a map on the ground and mark all the areas for the various activities?
4. Would they like to make things using the recyclable materials found at home?

> **Goals Achieved**
> - Enhanced imagination
> - Better visualization
> - Improved analytical thinking
> - Better ability to reformulate information
> - Enhanced creative thinking

Tick-tack Tips
1. Provide the children with recyclable material to visualize, analyse, reformulate, plan and create their own playground!
2. Take them to a junkyard; you can keep them creatively occupied during their summer vacations.

Synthesize and Reformulate

Activity—13

Zero Gravity on Earth!

RESOURCES REQUIRED
- Colour pencils
- A drawing sheet

Getting Ready:
1. Spare some time to have long and creative conversations with the children about why things that fall.
2. Give the children their stationery.

Proposed Situation:
You are on a family holiday and your children have decided to play basketball every day. Suddenly, they see a group of people gathering around a portable television, discussing something very seriously. Your children, too, want to be a part of the discussion. They instantly switch on the television and quickly browse through the channels, but fail to notice anything that grabs their attention. Just when they were about to turn off the television, they hear 'BREAKING NEWS' that the earth will lose its gravity for the next two days!

Tickle the Thoughts:
1. Ask the children what will happen to the earth, the people

Being a Brilliant Thinker

living on it, the plants, animals, birds and the aquatic life if the earth loses its gravity.
2. Ask them if Superman will need extra superpowers to fly around the earth.
3. What will happen to the apples when they fall off the tree.
4. How will they restore gravity?

Goals Achieved
- Enhanced abstract thinking
- Better creative thinking
- Improved analytical thinking

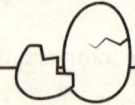

Tick-tack Tips
1. Gravity is the natural force that pulls any object or a body towards the centre of the earth or towards any other physical body having mass. It causes things to fall towards the earth. Anything that has mass also has a gravitational pull. The more the mass of the object, the stronger is the gravitational pull. The earth's gravity is what keeps from floating into the space.
2. Zero gravity, also called Zero-G, refers to the state or condition of weightlessness. It is the opposite of gravity.
3. Zero-G could be your next holiday with the children to one of the fancy amusement parks! Remember to carry a weighing scale!

Activity—14

Flying Apples!

RESOURCES REQUIRED
- Colour pencils
- A notebook

Getting Ready:

1. Spare some time to have long and creative conversations with children during their air travel to their grandparent's house. Talk to them about how the airplane takes off against the gravity to fly into the sky where they can see only the blue sky and the beautiful clouds.
2. Hand over the stationery to the children.

Proposed Situation:

You are taking your children to their grandparent's house for a holiday by an airplane. On boarding the plane, your daughter starts arguing with your son over the window seat to get a better view of the clouds. However, he manages to win the argument. He quickly fastens his seat belts and the flight takes off. As he is busy admiring the colours in the sky, he suddenly notices beautiful red apples flying around the airplane!

56 Being a Brilliant Thinker

Tickle the Thoughts:

1. Ask your children who do they think put the apples on the clouds.
2. How do they think apples got there?
3. What do they think has happened on earth that all the apples are floating in air?
4. What will happen if the apples fly into the space? Will the astronauts make a fruit punch or a nice apple pie for the evening?

🎯 Goals Achieved
- Enhanced abstract thinking
- Better creative thinking
- Improved analytical thinking
- Enhanced critical thinking

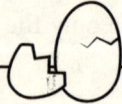

Tick-tack Tips
1. Encourage the children to evaluate what they see. Not everything that is visible is always true.
2. Can you base this situation on any kind of scientific fact or finding or research?

Activity–15

Yapping Utensils and the Smart Bin!

RESOURCES REQUIRED
- Colour pencils
- A notebook

Getting Ready:
1. Spare some time to have long, creative and funny conversations with children. When someone is cooking or washing the utensils in the kitchen, ask the children to listen to the sounds coming from the kitchen. Tell them to imagine that the utensils could talk.
2. Give the required stationery to the children.

Proposed Situation:

One day, the utensils in the kitchen were talking and giggling at the sad Bin who is always full of garbage. Mr Bin looked at all his friends in the kitchen who were washed and sparkling clean. Sleepy and upset, he walked out of the kitchen and slept at the door. When Mr Bin woke up in the morning, he saw himself transformed into a smart mechanized garbage incinerator! 'Was it magic?' Mr Bin wondered.

Being a Brilliant Thinker

Tickle the Thoughts:

1. What do your children think happened during the magic?
2. Write down the new features of Mr Bin. Can you draw a smart mechanized garbage incinerator?
3. If the children were the magician who turned Mr Bin into an incinerator, what additional features would they like to add to it?
4. Can they think of a fairy tale which had utensils that could talk?

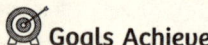

Goals Achieved
- Better ability to synthesize and reformulate idea
- Improved abstract thinking
- Enhanced creative thinking

Tick-tack Tips
1. This activity encourages children to synthesize and reformulate valuable information to arrive at a comprehensive analysis, which they can put to test.
2. You may float ideas such as the bin extends its arms to pick all the trash and puts them into its belly or pour water over the noisy utensils making a racket.

Activity—16

The Shower in the Bathroom!

RESOURCES REQUIRED
► Recyclable materials

Getting Ready:

This activity will require you and the child to search for recyclable material at the spur of the moment. Prepare in advance and keep a few materials handy so that the child can pick according to what he or she wants to make.

Proposed Situation:

Your child has just returned from the football training, sweaty and tired. You are cooking in the kitchen; your husband is yet to return from work and your older son is listening to music. You ask your child to quickly take a shower. As he or she soaps the body and tries to turn on the shower, it does not work.

Tickle the Thoughts:

1. Is there a problem with the shower or have you run out of water?
2. How can your child call for help?

Situation Continues:

Knowing that there is nobody around who can hear your child's cry for help, he or she screams with all his or her might, and you come to the rescue. You fill a big bucket of water and your child finally takes a bath. Now that he or she is out of the bathroom, your child says that there is a problem with the shower. The child calls the plumber to fix it, but finds out that the plumber is unavailable for the next two days! Both of you plan to fix the shower all yourself! Your child asks his or her brother for help. The child takes off the cover of the shower and cleans the sedimentation that had deposited at its mouth and puts it back. However, it still does not seem to work. So, he or she asks the brother for his help to make a new shower with the resources available at home!

Tickle the Thoughts:

1. Ask the children what materials they will require to make the shower.
2. Ask them if they have all the required resources available at home.
3. Plan and list the resources that they will need to procure from the hardware shop.
4. Ask them if they would like to add new features in terms of design to the shower? Tell them to draw it.
5. Ask them to think of the method to make a shower.

Goals Achieved
- Enhanced problem-solving abilities
- Improved creative thinking
- Better applying and testing abilities
- Improved planning ability

Activity–16

Tick-tack Tip

This activity encourages the children to synthesize and reformulate information such that children can create a new shower with the help of their analysis.

Activity–17

Device for My Trek to the Jungle!

Getting Ready:
Give the required stationery to the children to create a device.

Proposed Situation:
Your child wants to go trekking with his or her friends into the jungle, and you are apprehensive about the dangers they might encounter!

Tickle the Thoughts:
1. Ask them what could the possible dangers in the jungle be.
2. What precautionary measures should they take to keep themselves safe?
3. Propose the idea of a walkie-talkie to the children and ask them to think about the required resources for the device.
4. Ask them about other possible devices they can make to share their locations.

> **Goals Achieved**
> - Improved abstract thinking
> - Improved analytical thinking
> - Enhanced creative thinking
> - Better critical thinking

Activity–17   63

Tick-tack Tips
1. Ask the children to explore different safety devices and help them understand the importance of those devices.
2. Share information regarding the special clothes the soldiers wear and the equipment they carry—camouflage suit, specialized helmets with night vision glasses, Global Positioning System (GPS) devices, etc.

Activity–18

Hi-Tech Shoes!

RESOURCES REQUIRED
- Shoes
- A glue gun
- A thermometer

Getting Ready:

Keep the resources ready for the children to begin work.

Proposed Situation:

Your child's school has organized a rock climbing camp and your children are excited to go with their friends. The camp is next week and they have seven days to prepare for it.

Tickle the Thoughts:

1. Ask your children to make a list of things he or she should carry to the camp.
2. Ask them how they can avoid carrying heavy bags.
3. Ask them what features they would like to add to their shoes to avoid slipping.

Goals Achieved
- Improved abstract thinking
- Increased analytical thinking
- Enhanced creative thinking

Tick-tack Tips

1. Mentioned below are the things the children may need to be informed about:
   a) Navigation: Map, compass and GPS
   b) Sun Protection: Sunscreen, lip balm and goggles/glacier goggles
   c) Insulation/Clothing: Fleece jacket, vests and pants, insulation jackets, hats, socks, gloves, mittens, hiking gaiters, scarves, waterproof jackets and pants
   d) Illumination: Flash lights with extra batteries
   e) Fire Starter: Emergency survival fire
   f) Kit: Multi-tool kit, duct tape
   g) Nutrition: Extra days food supply, nuts and chocolates
   h) Hydration: Water bottles (insulated)
   i) Emergency Shelter: Reflective blanket, bivvy, tents (emergency shelter used by hikers/mountaineers)
   j) First Aid Supplies: Antiseptic lotions, BZK wipes, assorted adhesive bandages, adhesive wound closure strips, gauze pads, pain killers, antihistamines, splinters, safety pins
   k) Equipment: Route guide, rope, ice axe, crampons, pulley, shovels, prusik cords, avalanche transceiver, signalling mirror

Activity–19

Surprise Trip to the Space!

RESOURCES REQUIRED
- A pen
- A paper

Getting Ready:

Before the little astronauts take a trip into outer space, ask them to write down, from their imagination, what they might see.

Proposed Situation:

You plan a trip with your children to the space centre in your city. However, your child contests that none of his or her friends' parents take their children to the space centre for a holiday. He or she says, 'I wish I could have gone to an amusement park and had some fun there.'

Since it is a holiday today and you have some extra time in hand, you sit with your child, as he or she reluctantly examines the details of the space centre. Your child is presently surprised, as it is an actual space centre from where REAL satellites are launched! 'Ah! Is this a dream?' your child asks you.

You are all excited about your holiday. Your child talks about it with his or her friends every day. You have asked your child to read articles and listen to the latest news. In the classroom, your child reads a new chapter about space museums, and he or she already knows some facts about the museum, and his or her friends don't even have a clue! Your child, now, is hailed as a 'genius'.

Finally, the day arrives when you are standing at the gate of the space centre with your children—your child's dream holiday destination! He or she rushes to the gate and excitedly asks for the printed copy of the gate pass. The chief security officer gently asks your child for his or her identification card. He or she hands them over to the officer, and he ushers them inside the huge compound, where a towering structure stands majestically with fascinating displays around it. Suddenly, you hear an announcement: 'The executive authorities at the space centre are taking three children to space. The guided week-long trip to space is precisely after 4 weeks.'

Your child wants to grab this opportunity to live his or her dream of going to space for a week! He or she is thrilled and looks at you expectantly for your consent! Your husband looks at you through his spectacles. You are concerned about your child's safety. You look at your child and feel that he or she is feeling disappointed, and suddenly both of you say 'yes' together. Your child thanks both of you and promises to be an obedient child forever.

You take him or her to the administration office to register for the trip. The administration officer informs you that the training will begin in seven days. All is done, and very soon, your child is going to be the youngest astronaut in the world!

Tickle the Thoughts:

1. Ask the child to list out the things they are going to carry with them to space.
2. Ask the children what they think will be taught during the training.
3. What souvenirs they would like to bring back to earth?

Being a Brilliant Thinker

🎯 Goals Achieved
- Enhanced abstract thinking
- Improved analytical thinking
- Better creative thinking
- Enhanced critical thinking

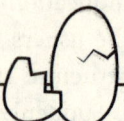

Tick-tackTips
1. Space centres provide rich learning experiences.
2. The Vikram Sarabhai Space Centre (VSSC) is located in Thiruvananthapuram, Kerala. It is a space research centre of the Indian Space Research Organization (ISRO) that focusses on India's satellite programmes.
3. Taking the children for a summer vacation to an educational destination will give them the opportunity to experience knowledge. Allow them to imagine the unimaginable.

Activity–20

Wounded Animal on the Road!

Proposed Situation:

It is a beautiful morning, and you are preparing your child for school. You urge your child that you will be dropping him or her to school. On hearing this, your child is thrilled and is ready to leave for school. He or she is wearing a clean school uniform, shoes are sparkling clean, the bag is packed, and the water bottle is ready. Both of you are in the car and on your way to the school.

Your child tells you how excited he or she is about the day at school. Suddenly, you see the car just ahead of you go off the track, and you hear a little puppy cry. You halt the car on the side of the road and step out of it immediately to find out if anyone is hurt while you ask your child to go look for the puppy. You inform your child that you are going to help the people in the car and that the well-being of the puppy is in his or her hands.

Tickle the Thoughts:

1. How will your child help the puppy?
2. Can he or she get first aid for the puppy?
3. Which is the closest hospital?
4. Ask them if their Dad has a veterinarian's number on his cell.

Being a Brilliant Thinker

🎯 Goals Achieved
- Enhanced memory and association
- Improved understanding and problem-solving abilities
- Better sequential (linear) thinking
- Improved critical thinking

Tick-tack Tips

1. Share information **with the** children:
   a) An injured animal is likely to be in shock. Approach the animal with necessary caution. It might bite or scratch you to defend itself. Observe if it is still aggressive and only then move closer. Maintain eye contact, wait until it has calmed down and lets you go closer.
   b) Gently stroke the animal, look for the collar to find its name, or call out the name in case you know it.
   c) Check if the animal is conscious by gently tapping near the inner corner of its eye.
   d) Check if the animal is bleeding; cover the wounds with a clean cloth.
   e) Check the pulse of the animal.
   f) Removing the animal from the accident site can be very tricky, as we do not want to cause further injuries to the animal. You may slide a blanket under the body of the animal to lift it. If you think the animal has broken bones, use the removable shelf behind the back seat of the car; the parcel shelf can be used as a makeshift stretcher to move the animal from the accident site.

Activity–20 71

g) Stay calm and take the animal to the nearest hospital. While you are on your way, inform the hospital in advance that you are bringing in an emergency.

Activity–21

Food for All!

Proposed Situation:

It is the day your child waits for all year long—his or her birthday! You have organized a surprise birthday party at your child's favourite hangout. His or her friends have been invited and they have brought a lot of gifts. A scrumptious meal has been laid out for everyone to enjoy. After the party was over, your child's friends left for their homes. You are ready to leave as well, and ask your child to get his or her belongings. Your child goes to the area where the food had been laid out and notices that a lot of it is lying around. Your child brings his or her belongings to you and mentions to you about the wastage of food.

On your way back home, the car halts at the traffic light, you casually turn around and notice your child looking at a family of four, begging for alms. He or she is looking at the father; he is sitting on his haunches; the mother is begging with a baby in her arms, and a young boy is sitting on the road side and crying bitterly for food!

Tickle the Thoughts:

1. Ask the child what they plan on doing with the leftover food.
2. Ask them if there is anything that they can do to feed the poor so that no child sleeps with an empty stomach.

Activity–21 73

🎯 Goals Achieved
- Enhanced memory and association techniques
- Increase ability to synthesize and reformulate information
- Improved understanding and problem-solving abilities
- Improved analytical thinking
- Better sequential (linear) thinking
- Enhanced critical thinking

Tick-tack Tips
1. Tell the children to avoid wastage of food.
2. Encourage them to think empathetically about people who cannot afford food and go to bed with an empty stomach at night.
3. Share information about various organizations that collect surplus food from the hotels and feed the underprivileged.

Apply and Test

Activity–22

Cheater Cock!

Proposed Situation:

It is the time of the year when your children study hard. They have revised for the exams, and are all set to take on them. They get their question paper and begin to write all the answers carefully. Time flies, and they are already halfway through the question paper. Suddenly, they hear someone whisper their name. As they look up, they see their friend making absurd gestures. That is when they realize that the friend is asking for their answer sheets. Your children's faces turn pale at the thought of being caught by the teacher!

Tickle the Thoughts:

1. Ask the child what they should do—help the friend with the answers and take the risk of being caught.
2. Should they tell the teacher about their friend's behaviour?

Goals Achieved
- Improved understanding and problem-solving abilities
- Improved analytical thinking
- Better sequential (linear) thinking
- Enhanced critical thinking

Being a Brilliant Thinker

Tick-tack Tip

It is a good idea to be consistent with studies throughout the year. Encourage children to think that they have prepared well for the exams, and they will not need to cheat.

Activity—23

Dino in the Town!

RESOURCES REQUIRED
- 1 box of colour pencils
- A paper

Getting Ready:

Keep the required stationery ready before the children to begin work.

Proposed Situation:

You are taking your child to your parents' house. It is a long and tiring drive. Your child has already read his or her favourite storybook, and now he or she is looking out of the window. You are driving past the countryside, and there is not much traffic. The sun is shining bright and the pleasant breeze is making your child feel sleepy. Suddenly, the child notices a giant, unusual animal walking fearlessly past your car and your child begins to wonder what it is. You look at each other equally shocked. He or she asks you whether you saw the monstrous animal or if it was all a dream. You tell him or her that it was a dinosaur!

Tickle the Thoughts:

1. Ask the child if the dinosaur was real.

2. Ask him or her how did it come back to life.
3. Whom does he or she inform?
4. Ask the children to write and draw about his or her experience.

Goals Achieved
- Improved memory and association
- Enhanced analytical thinking
- Improved critical thinking
- Better understanding and problem-solving abilities

Tick-tack Tips

1. Information sharing:

Geologists have traditionally divided the 4,600 million years of earth to the present day into a series of standard time zones. The major divisions of the history of the earth are called 'eras'. Each era is sub-divided into smaller time zones called 'periods'. Each period is further divided into smaller divisions called 'ages'.

Dinosaurs lived in the Mesozoic Era, which is divided into the Triassic, Jurassic and Cretaceous Periods.
The 'era of the dinosaurs' is divided into three categories traditionally based on the geographical timescale:
Triassic Period: 250 to 200 million years ago
Jurassic Period: 200 to 145 million years ago
Cretaceous Period: 145 to 65 million years ago

2. Why did dinosaurs go extinct?

A large asteroid or a comet about 11 to 81 kilometres and 6.8 to 50.3 miles in diameter hit the earth about 66 million years ago. The Chicxulub crater is an impact crater buried underneath the Yucatán Peninsula in Mexico. Its centre is located near the town of Chicxulub after which the carter is named. The violent collision triggered tsunamis across the oceans, causing powerful earthquakes and releasing enough heat to start many fires. Due to the impact, materials went up into the air and descended as acid rain. A thick blanket of dust that was thrown up darkened the globe, affecting plants and other photosynthesizing life and consequently, dinosaurs became extinct.

Activity—24

Zero Pollution Day!

RESOURCES REQUIRED
- 1 box of colour pencils
- A paper

Getting Ready:

Keep the required stationery ready before the children begin work.

Proposed Situation:

It is an extended weekend, and you are heading out with your family for shopping. The children are ready, but you are yet to prepare lunch. You switch on the television for your children and hand them the remote control. As they browse through the channels to hear what is happening in the world, something catches their attention. They hear that today the government has announced that petrol-driven vehicles are banned from hitting the roads every Sunday and they realize that it is SUNDAY TODAY!

Tickle the Thoughts:

1. Ask the children why the government took this decision?
2. Will the decision benefit anybody?
3. Ask them how they can go for shopping.
4. Ask them to suggest an alternative to fuel-driven vehicles.

Activity–24 83

5. Ask them what will happen if they were to go to school riding a horse.
6. Ask them about car pools and why is it a good idea to have car pools. Also, ask them about the safety precautions they should take while travelling with strangers.

Goals Achieved
- Enhanced memory and association techniques
- Enhanced analytical thinking
- Better critical thinking
- Improved understanding and problem-solving abilities

Tick-tack Tips
1. By now, pollution and its effects have been already introduced to children. Encourage them to design new alternatives to save the planet from being polluted.
2. Encourage them to take initiatives to organize car pools for going to a friend's birthday party. Allow them to call their friends by giving them the monitored access to phone for organizing the trip. It will also enhance their skills of talking on the phone.

Activity—25

Environment Summit!

RESOURCES REQUIRED
- A pen
- A paper

Getting Ready:

While you are driving, share information on pollution with your children. Show them the fuel emission from the cars, trucks, factories, etc.

Proposed Situation:

The people on the planet have vowed to free it from pollution, and the United Nations has cordially invited your child to a notable summit to share his or her valuable opinion. Your child has to prepare a motivational speech that will give the intelligent audience something to think about and pledge their support to a pollution free planet.

Tickle the Thoughts:

1. Ask the child to list out how he or she will prepare for the summit.
2. What all topics should he or she stress upon during the speech?

3. How will he or she motivate the lazy audience to proactively pledge to a pollution free planet?
4. What are the solutions he or she will offer to spread the message to the world around?

Goals Achieved
- Enhanced memory and association techniques
- Improved analytical thinking
- Enhanced critical thinking
- Better understanding and problem-solving abilities
- Improved communication and presentation skills

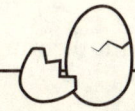

Tick-tack Tips
1. Share information with the children about various topics to be addressed in his or her speech such as marine litter and microplastics, how to prevent and reduce air pollution, cut out lead poisoning from paint and batteries, protect water-based ecosystems from pollution, ways to deal with soil pollution. Support them to discuss the expenditure involved in saving the planet.
2. Once the child has prepared the speech, have a family gathering where the child can deliver the speech. Encourage the child by praising his or her speech. The family meeting can be followed by the child's favourite snacks.

Activity–26

Road Safety Rules!

RESOURCES REQUIRED
- A pen
- A paper

Getting Ready:

Go for a drive with your children and discuss with them traffic rules, road safety measures, etc.

Proposed Situation:

Your child has been invited to his or her friend's pyjama party and he or she is super excited.

The father is dropping him or her to the friend's place. Your child embraces you with a warm hug and goodnight kisses before hopping into the car and fastening his or her seat belt.

As the car stops at the traffic signal, your child gets restless thinking about all the fun the party entails.

However, the father, to inculcate proper civic sense into the child, abides by the traffic rules.

Suddenly, you and your child see a white car zoom past, nearly missing the old man crossing the road!

Activity-26 87

Tickle the Thoughts:

1. Ask the child why do we have traffic signals.
2. What do the traffic signals mean?
3. Are the road safety rules only for the pedestrians or for everyone on the road?
4. Ask the child to list out the safety rules that they follow every day.
5. Urge the child to recommend the safety rules that they feel are important. Draw relevant designs to depict the new rules.

Goals Achieved:
- Enhanced analytical thinking
- Better critical thinking
- Improved understanding and problem-solving abilities

Tick-tackTips

1. Safety and security of the child should be given utmost priority. Most preventable accidents happen due to someone being careless—while either driving or crossing the road. We must make our children aware of their safety and that of others on the road.

2. The various kinds of people on the road are:
   a) Pedestrians
   b) Cyclists
   c) Motorists
   d) Passengers of vehicles like car, bus and tram

3. Inform the children about:
    a) Local road
    b) Preferred route
    c) Signals
    d) Paying attention, removing earphones while walking or driving
    e) Using sidewalks
    f) Crossing the road at the pedestrian crossing and not where the road bends

Activity–27

Bus Safety Rules!

Proposed Situation:

It is a beautiful Monday morning and your children are all set to attend school and meet their friends. Your children are thrilled to share their stories of how they enjoyed spending time with their cousins over the weekend. As the school bus arrives, all the children run towards the bus to board it. All of a sudden, one of your child's friends falls off the bus onto the road. Just then, a car brushes against him, leaving him shocked and slightly wounded.

Tickle the Thoughts:

1. Ask the child why their friend fell off the school bus.
2. Ask them what could have happened to their dear friend.
3. What safety rules they must follow diligently while travelling in public or private transport?

Goals Achieved
- Improved sequential thinking
- Better analytical thinking
- Improved critical thinking
- Better understanding and problem-solving abilities

Being a Brilliant Thinker

Tick-tack Tips

1. Children travel to school by bus. Safety of the child is a paramount concern of the schools and parents. It is imperative for them to be informed and abide by the safety rules.

2. Safety rules for boarding a bus:
   a) Arrive at the bus stop 5 minutes prior to the arrival of the bus. Never run to or from the bus stop.
   b) Wait at the designated bus stop in a secure place, away from the road.
   c) If you need to cross the street to board the bus, wait for the traffic lights to turn red before crossing the street.
   d) Let the bus come to a complete stop before you board the bus.
   e) Hold on to the handrails as you board the bus.
   f) Do not push or shove.

3. Safety rules for riding the bus:
   a) Take your seat and sit facing the front.
   b) Place your school bag either on your lap or under your seat.
   c) Do not rest your elbow in a way that it sticks out of the window.
   d) Do not throw trash inside or outside the bus, as it may either distract the driver or injure a pedestrian on the road.

e) Talk softly as the driver needs to concentrate on navigating through the traffic. Fighting or shouting distracts the bus driver.
f) Maintain silence when approaching a railroad crossing.
g) Introduce your child to the bus evacuation drills.

4. Rules for de-boarding the bus safely:
   a) Remain in the seat until the bus comes to a complete stop. Remain calm. Do not push.
   b) If a friend is in a hurry to get off the bus, allow him or her to go ahead. The bus driver will not leave without dropping you off at the bus stop, and of course, the parent (or the person responsible to get the child home from the bus stop) will be waiting for you.
   c) When you are about to get off the bus, hold the handrails.
   d) Once you have alighted from the bus, wait for the bus to leave. Else, walk away from the bus; make sure the bus driver can see you crossing the road. Look on both sides of the road for incoming traffic and traffic signals.
   e) If you happen to drop something close to the bus, do not pick it up. Inform an adult. *Always remember that if you cannot see the driver, the driver cannot see you.*

Activity–28

Personal Safety Rules!

Proposed Situation:

You are planning to go on a business tour for two days. Since your children are now responsible enough to take care of themselves properly, you ask them about their plans to spend their time with the caretaker.

Tickle the Thoughts:

1. Ask your children to prepare a comprehensive list of the ways they will ensure their safety and security.
2. What valuable information should they keep in mind while you are away?

> ### 🎯 Goals Achieved
> - Improved sequential thinking
> - Enhanced analytical thinking
> - Better critical thinking
> - Better understanding and problem-solving ideas

Activity—28

Tick-tack Tips

1. Constantly watching over children's every move may not be possible even when you are at home. Having said that, keep in mind the following rules:

   a) Ask the child to not open the door to strangers and encourage them to keep personal information to themselves.

   b) Make a list of emergency phone numbers and get it laminated. Ensure that everything can be clearly read on it. Add your name, address and other necessary details, and ask your children to memorize them. Put it up at a visible place.

   c) Ensure that the children are in a position to use the safety system in case of emergency. For example, they should know how to operate the lift in case they get stuck in it.

   d) Establish the rules for using the medicine box with the children. Overdose or unintentionally consuming the medicines can be dangerous.

   e) Restricted Area: If the furniture has edges or are placed in a way that they jut out, it can pose a safety threat for the child.

   Outdoor Safety:

   a) Restricted Area: Mark the area where the child is not allowed to go as it houses potential danger.

   b) Allergy: Inform the children about the foods, plants, etc., that may cause allergies, and what should they do if they get one.

c) Do not ingest anything given by a stranger. Discipline them to say no to temptations.
d) No one should touch the child's body. The child has to be taught to say a loud and clear 'NO' to anybody attempting to touch him or her.
e) Do not do anything if it does not feel right.
f) Stay away from the fire.
g) If lost in a mall, go cautiously to the check out the section of the mall to seek help. Show them the administration section of a mall from where official announcements are promptly issued.
h) Establish specific guidelines for operating communal bathrooms, including how to carefully check for hidden cameras.

Activity–29

Stuck in the Lift!

RESOURCES REQUIRED
- A pen
- A paper

Proposed Situation:

You picked up your child from his or her friend's place and dropped him or her home. You live on the fifth floor. Your child presses the button to call the lift to the ground floor.

Tring! The lift's door opens and an elderly woman walks out of it. He or she greets the woman and walks into the lift. There is no one else in the lift. Your child presses the number 5 for the fifth floor. The lift begins to move.

Suddenly, it stops in between the second and the third floor!

Tickle the Thoughts:

1. Ask the child what must have happened.
2. Who is the closest person that your child can reach out to?
3. How should your child call for help?
4. Ask the child if there are any instructions to call for help in the lift. Is there a lift-manual in the lift?

Goals Achieved
- Improved sequential (linear) thinking
- Better analytical thinking
- Enhanced critical thinking
- Better understanding and problem-solving abilities

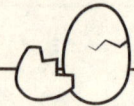

Tick-tack Tip

It is important for the child to remain calm while he or she is still stuck in the lift. Think positively until help arrives. Try to balance a spinning ball on your index finger to keep yourself distracted.

Activity–30

Fire Safety!

Proposed Situation:

You have taken your children to their grandparents' house over the weekend. Grandma has just finished offering prayers and has gone to sprinkle holy water all around the house. You are busy preparing dinner and your husband has gone to buy groceries. Your child is alone in the pooja room.

Suddenly, he or she sees the towel next to the mandir has caught fire.

Tickle the Thoughts:

1. Ask the child what he or she would do.
2. How do you think the towel caught fire?
3. How will you instantly extinguish the fire?

> **Goals Achieved**
> - Better sequential (linear) thinking
> - Improved analytical thinking
> - Better critical thinking
> - Enhanced understanding and problem-solving abilities

Being a Brilliant Thinker

Tick-tack Tips
1. It is important for the child to remain calm, while quick thinking remains the key to safety. Share the below-mentioned information with the children to help them confront the situation when it arises. In the first place, children should be introduced to non-negotiable safety rules. Next, they should be instructed how to escape the fire.
    - It is imperative for not only the schools to practice fire drills with the school students and staff, but also for the family to practice fire drills at home. The fire safety rules may remain the same, but for young children to know the escape routes and other safety rules will be different for various locations.
    - Do not play with matches or lighters.
    - Run the extinguished matches under water to ensure it has been extinguished before discarding it.
    - Never leave candles or incense sticks burning.
    - Do not leave cell phones on charging overnight.
    - Keep flammable objects away from burners and stoves.
    - Encourage them to understand what does 'escape' mean and mark the escape route for the house. Furthermore, mark the safest assembly point for the entire family.
    - Place fire extinguishers at the level where the child can access it. Also, ensure they know how to operate it. If you demonstrate it, it is simple to operate; they should be able to operate it independently. Ensure that the fire extinguisher has not expired and replace it whenever required.
    - Use the windows to escape but first carefully touch the door or window to examine for heat.
    - In case their clothes catch fire, they must stop, drop and roll on the floor to extinguish the fire. Do it yourself to demonstrate it to the children.

Activity–31

Watch in the Aquarium!

Proposed Situation:

You have brought a new aquarium home, and you are very excited to show it to the children. They are thrilled to see the beautiful and colourful fishes inside it. You ask them to look for an exotic fish in the aquarium. They notice that the oxygen pump in the aquarium is not working properly. One of your children is tempted to check it. He or she puts his or her hand into the aquarium. Suddenly, his or her watch slips off the wrist and falls into the aquarium!

Tickle the Thoughts:

1. Ask them how they can remove the watch from the aquarium given its size.
2. Encourage the children to design a peculiar device that can be used to remove the watch from the aquarium. Moreover, examine the device before employing it inside the aquarium.
3. How will you remove the water from the watch so that it works?

Goals Achieved

- Improved sequential (linear) thinking
- Enhanced analytical thinking
- Better critical thinking
- Better ability to synthesize and reformulate ideas
- Improved abilities of application and testing
- Enhanced analysing and evaluating abilities
- Better understanding and problem-solving abilities

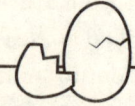

Tick-tack Tip

To increase the complexity of the ingenious device, you may carefully specify the essential items to develop the device such as a stick, rubber band and a string. Encourage them to examine the device if it works effectively.

Activity—32

Blind Person Crossing the Road!

Proposed Situation:

You are taking your children to the local shopping centre near your house. It is a regular evening, and the traffic is moving fast. As you are waiting at the traffic signal to turn green, your children notice an old man standing at the zebra crossing, waiting for the signal. He is wearing black glasses and has a white walking stick. Your children ask you what he is waiting for. You tell them that he is a blind person waiting to cross the road!

Tickle the Thoughts:

1. Tell the child how they can identify a blind person.
2. Explain to them how he will cross the road.
3. Ask them if they need your help.
4. Are there enough provisions made for blind people to cross roads?
5. What provisions or devices they would design to help the blind move independently and safely?

Being a Brilliant Thinker

Goals Achieved
- Enhanced analytical thinking
- Better critical thinking
- Increase ability to synthesize and reformulate information
- Improved abilities of application and testing
- Enhanced analysing and evaluating abilities
- Better understanding and problem-solving abilities

Tick-tack Tip

It is significant for the children to appreciate the importance of offering help with empathy and not out of pity! Take them to a school for the blind and show the children how capable and enthusiastic the children studying there are. You could also take them to a school for children with disabilities and help them recognize the qualities they possess such as using their feet or mouth to paint. It is indeed a beautiful and very moving experience. Therefore, ensure you brief your children well before you take them through these enriching experiences.

Analyse and Evaluate

Activity—33

A Visit to an Old-age Home!

Proposed Situation:

You are planning to take your children to visit their grandaunt, who stays at an old-age home. You have just explained to them that it is a place for old people who live together as they are now unable to live with their families. Such facilities are called old-age homes. You inform the children that their grandaunt has many hilarious stories to tell and has a great sense of humour! You ask them if they should persuade her to stay at your home for the weekend. Your children are thrilled by the idea and make a beautiful invitation card for her. You give them an envelope for the card to write their grandaunt's name. You have arrived at the old-age home and are waiting for your aunt, with the children, at the reception.

Tickle the Thoughts:

1. Ask the children why old people don't live with their families now.
2. Who leaves them at the old-age home? Is it good to leave the elderly at old-age homes against their wishes?
3. Are they taken care of at such homes?
4. Old people are fun to be with! Is it possible to adopt people from the old-age home?

106 Being a Brilliant Thinker

5. Ask them what is the biggest takeaway from their trip to the old-age home?

Goals Achieved
- Better critical thinking
- Enhanced analysing and evaluating abilities
- Better understanding and problem-solving abilities

Tick-tack Tip

Introduce the children to the names of organizations that offer good care to old people. Also, make them understand that the elderly need both love and care to lead a healthy life.

Activity—34

Lost during a Jungle Safari!

Proposed Situation:

Your children are going on a Jungle Safari. This is the first time you are taking your children to see a sanctuary. All your bookings are done. Your children are excited to see the animals. As you reach the main entrance of the sanctuary, they see many people rushing towards it. Your children also rush towards the entrance to show their passes to the officer at the window. You lose sight of your children in the crowd. By now, they have boarded the train that they thought would take them on the jungle safari. As they settle down on their seats, the train begins to move, and they realize their parents are not with them.

Tickle the Thoughts:

1. Ask the children how they will find you.
2. Ask them how can they find out where you are.
3. Whom should they reach out for help?

> **Goals Achieved**
> - Better critical thinking
> - Enhanced analysing and evaluating abilities
> - Better understanding and problem-solving abilities

Being a Brilliant Thinker

Tick-tack Tips
1. Before taking them on a jungle safari, talk to them about their safety and security. Also, inform them about the local people who can be approached for help.
2. It is a brilliant idea for the children to wear identity cards, which carry your contact numbers, whenever you take them for such outings.

Activity—35

Lost in the Jungle!

Proposed Situation:

It is the time of the year when your children's exams are over, and they are all set for the summer vacation to begin. You are going to visit your sister who lives in a village near the jungle. It is a glorious sunny day, and your children are playing football with their cousins. One of the cousins kicks the ball hard and it flies into the jungle. Your child decides to go into the jungle to look for the ball. After a while, the child realizes that he or she is lost in the jungle!

Tickle the Thoughts:

1. Ask them how the child will find his or her way back home.
2. Ask them where you can find the child in the jungle.
3. Ask them in which direction you should head to find help.
4. How can you signal your child about your location in the jungle?
5. Ask them how they will endure until help arrives. What can he or she eat or not eat in the jungle? How should he or she avoid dehydration?

Being a Brilliant Thinker

> **Goals Achieved**
> - Better critical thinking
> - Enhanced analysing and evaluating abilities
> - Better understanding and problem-solving abilities

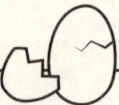

Tick-tack Tip

1. Encourage the children to determine survival techniques such as:
   a) A source of water such as a river or a stream flowing through the jungle. Civilization is principally around a water source.
   b) Consuming things that animals such as monkeys would eat
   c) Staying away from mushrooms and white and yellow berries
   d) Leaving clear marks of your presence at a visible place, such as a flag made of a thick stick and a leftover piece of cloth or polythene bag
   e) Travelling downhill will help the child find civilization

Activity–36

Lost in the Ocean!

Proposed Situation:

You have planned a boating trip for your children. It is a long drive to the boating site. Your children are bored and look out of the window. You notice that the children have dozed off. You wake them up and tell them that they have reached the site. Once they are up, one of the children tells you that he or she had been dreaming about a boat drifting in a lake all alone.

Tickle the Thoughts:

1. Ask the child how they think the boat in their dream got there.
2. Ask them about the tools required for navigating across the ocean, and the technique to spot themselves on the map.
3. In case of an emergency during their boating trip, whom should they call for help?

Goals Achieved
- Better critical thinking
- Enhanced analysing and evaluating abilities
- Better understanding and problem-solving abilities

Tick-tack Tips

Encourage the children to think about the information mentioned below while boating.

a) Safety rules
- Stay alert all the time.
- Know how to swim (with and against the current).
- Always wear a life jacket.
- Never paddle alone, always go boating with a companion.
- Never overload the boat.
- Always check the weather before heading out.
- Check the boat for leaks before setting sail.
- Share information about the sea route with the children.
- Show the children the placement of the first aid kit and what should it consist of.

b) Survival techniques:
- Do not stand or walk when the current is strong.
- Float on your back with feet and arm extended.
- Float with feet pointed downstream.
- Carry extra food supplies.

Activity–37

Peels in the Park!

Proposed Situation:

You have planned a small picnic to the neighbouring garden for your children and their friends. They are carrying homemade food and fresh fruits. The children are having fun and sharing their food. One of the children notice that others are throwing the banana peels in the garden. Even though they feel embarrassed, they choose to ignore. Suddenly, they hear a loud cry followed by a thud. Everyone turns around to find an old woman lying on the ground and asking for help. She had slipped on one of the banana peels strewn around by the children.

Tickle the Thoughts:

1. Ask the children why did she fall.
2. Ask them who was responsible for her fall.
3. What should be done to avoid such accidents?

The Situation Continues:

Your child runs to the old woman and helps her stand up. The child escorts her to a nearby bench and apologizes to her for being irresponsible while the others are still busy with their mischief!

The elderly woman looks at the child and runs her wrinkled, soft hands on his or her forehead. She appreciates your child's

114 Being a Brilliant Thinker

help. She tells him or her that the child will be rewarded for the kindness.

The old woman gets up from the bench, shakes hands with your child, takes her walking stick, and begins to walk away.

Your child then realizes that he or she has something in his or her hand. He or she opens the fist to see a beautiful but crumpled silver colour paper. He or she straightens the crumpled paper carefully to read the message written on it.

'You are invited to the Chocolate Factory! The pass permits two people only!'

(The situation continues in the next activity.)

Goals Achieved
- Improved memory and associating abilities
- Better critical thinking
- Enhanced analysing and evaluating abilities
- Better understanding and problem-solving abilities

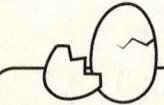

Tick-tackTips
1. Teach the children to be responsible for their actions. Show them how to properly dispose waste and the different kinds of dustbins for certain kinds of wastes.
2. Encourage the children to think about the moral behind the situation. Allow them to come up with their own versions of the situation.

Activity–38

Pass to the Chocolate Factory!

The Situation Continues:

The day of your child's visit to the Chocolate Factory is inching closer, and you know that his or her granny is very fond of chocolates. She has been secretly sharing a substantial portion of her chocolates with your child. You ask your child whom would he or she take along to the factory. Your child chooses his or her adorable Granny! Both of them are excited to visit the Chocolate Factory. Finally, the day that they had been waiting for has arrived!

Tickle the Thoughts:

1. Ask your child why the old woman in the garden rewarded him or her with the pass to the chocolate factory.
2. Ask your child what will he or she get to see at the factory.
3. If he or she was to design a chocolate factory, what are the things that the child would add to the design?
4. Ask the child what kind of chocolates he or she would like to make.

Being a Brilliant Thinker

Goals Achieved
- Enhanced abstract thinking abilities
- Improved divergent thinking abilities
- Better creative thinking abilities
- Increased analytical thinking abilities

Tick-tack Tips
1. Instil kindness and gratitude in children.
2. Encourage them to design a chocolate factory at home, using recyclable materials.

Activity–39

Fly with the Gas Balloons!

Proposed Situation:

Your child has been invited to his or her friend's birthday party. He or she wishes the friend and gives her a present. Your child is amazed to see how well the place has been decorated with beautiful lights; a huge table has been laid out with yummy food; and tattoo artists and cartoon characters are seen walking around. There is a long queue in front of the artists' stalls, but your child decides to go to the gas balloon stall. The sales boy is still busy setting it up, and he sees the child waiting for him. He is inflating the balloons, but he seems to be having trouble doing it. He is unable to hold on to so many balloons. Your child offers him help. The boy asks him or her to hold an odd bunch of gas balloons. Your child grabs the strings. Before your child could realize, the balloons lift him or her into the air, and up he or she goes!

Tickle the Thoughts:

1. Ask the child what made the child go up in the air.
2. How can the child get back to the ground?
3. How can he or she call for help?

Being a Brilliant Thinker

> **Goals Achieved**
> - Increased abstract thinking abilities
> - Better critical thinking abilities
> - Enhanced analyzing and evaluating abilities
> - Better understanding and problem-solving abilities

Tick-tack Tip
1. Share facts about balloons with the children:
   - A helium balloon rises up into the sky, the atmosphere. This is because each gas has its own weight. Helium is lighter than the weight of the air. The property is called Buoyancy.
   - The air in the atmosphere of the earth gets thinner as we go higher. The balloon can keep rising until the atmosphere surrounding the balloon possesses the same weight as helium in the balloon. This equal weight of the two gasses happens once the balloon reaches a height of 32 kilometres above the earth's surface.

Activity–40

Cousin's Wedding!

Proposed Situation:

The doorbell rings and you ask your child to check who it is. He or she looks through the magic eye and sees an old man who is often seen in the society with letters in his hands. Ah! It is the postman! Your child unlocks the door, and the postman hands over a beautiful envelope to him or her. The child thanks the postman and closes the door. He or she gives the envelope to the father and waits for him to open it. The child becomes more curious as the father opens the envelope.

The father looks at the child and tells him or her that it is an invitation to a cousin's wedding in Delhi, and all of them are going to attend it the coming week!

Tickle the Thoughts:

1. Ask the child why do people get married.
2. Ask them what they are going to do at the wedding.

Goals Achieved
- Better concrete thinking
- Enhanced convergent thinking
- Better sequential (linear) thinking

Tick-tack Tip

Family gatherings are an opportunity for children to meet the whole family. A child interacts with new members of the family and is a great social experience. It gives them a broader perspective and a deeper understanding of family values. Encourage them to interact by talking positively about the family.

Activity–41

Meeting a Mermaid!

Proposed Situation:

You are relaxing on the beach, watching the waves crash on the shore and feeling the gritty sand under your feet. The humid air is blowing through your hair. Your children are playing with a ball. Suddenly, they hear a child screaming. They quickly run towards the sound, spot another child in the water and get him safely to the shore. The concerned parents of the child are thankful to your children for being alert and helpful. They get back to the bench where you were sitting. Suddenly, they see a beautiful mermaid waving at them!

Tickle the Thoughts:

1. Ask your children who she is and from where did she come.
2. Ask the children what they are going to ask her.
3. If she grants them three wishes, what would the children wish for?

Goals Achieved
- Enhanced memory and association techniques
- Enhanced abstract thinking
- Increased divergent thinking
- Better creative thinking
- Improved analytical thinking

Tick-tack Tip

During the activity, encourage the children to perform good things for others and help them think about how they can inspire their friends to be good to others as well.

Activity–42

Visit to a Construction Site–I!

Proposed Situation:

You have planned to buy a new house and have asked your child to participate actively in the decision. You plan to visit a construction site with your child!

Tickle the Thoughts:

1. Ask the child what precautions they should take at the construction site.
2. Ask them to make a list of the things they need in the new house or room.

> **Goals Achieved**
> - Enhanced memory and association techniques
> - Enhanced abstract thinking
> - Increased convergent thinking
> - Improved critical thinking

Tick-tack Tip

Going to the construction site can be a great learning experience for the child. However, failures in identifying hazards are due to limited and improper training and ignorance on the workers' or management's side. Teach your children safety rules that they must follow at the construction site. You should also introduce site safety signs to your children. Following are a few safety hazards you must look out for:

- Tripping and falling
- Getting caught between objects
- Electrocutions
- Being struck by objects

Activity—42

Visit to a Construction Site–II!

Introduce the children to the following Site Safety Signs.

	Warning, Dangerous Site		Warning, Demolition work in progress
	Hard hats must be worn		No unauthorised person allowed
	Use ear protectors		Warning Look out for overhead loads
	High visibility vests should be worn		Children should not play on this site
	Protective footwear must be worn		No unauthorised access

Activity 6

Visit to a Construction Site–II

Introduce the children to the following site safety signs.

Warning, Dangerous zone		Warning, Demolition work in progress	
Hard hats must be worn	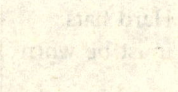	No entry to unauthorised persons allowed	
Dangerous machine		Warning, Trash must be removed from work area	
High visibility vest should be worn		Children should not play on this site	
Protective foot wear must be worn			

Evidence and Inference

Activity—43

Chocolate Rain!

Proposed Situation:

It is the rainy season and your children smell something nice. However, it is not the smell of the wet soil; it is the smell of something mouth-watering. The children are naturally wondering if the aunt next door is baking a cake or making chocolates.

While your children are sitting comfortably at their study table, looking out of the window and anticipating heavy rain, they see something trickling down the walls. They go closer to the window to get a better look.

As they go closer to the window, they witness a 'picturesque waterfall' of milk chocolate and roses made of chocolates in their garden! Instead of raindrops, they see that the roofs and the roads are covered with a blanket of icing sugar. They realize that they live in a fairyland!

Tickle the Thoughts:

1. Ask the children if it is really happening.
2. Ask them where the milk chocolate is flowing from.
3. Can they taste it?

Being a Brilliant Thinker

Goals Achieved
- Enhanced abstract thinking
- Better creative thinking
- Improved analytical thinking
- Enhanced critical thinking

Tick-tack Tips
1. Encourage the children to think of the hazards they might have to confront if they fail to think critically before ingesting the food or chocolates.
2. Ask them to come up with safety rules for food.

Activity—44

Mighty Wings to Fly!

Proposed Situation:

Your children's school has organized a trip to the bird sanctuary. They have been told to carry portable cameras, water bottles and hats. The children are also told to walk in a group.

Your children have seen and enjoyed watching numerous interesting birds and animals; migratory birds are one of them. Now, it is time for the birds to go back home. By the end of the trip, your children are tired and eager to go home. They board the school bus, and soon they are on their way back home! Your children take a shower, have their dinner, and go to bed.

Suddenly, they see an enormous bird flying towards them through their window. It comes inside, perches on the headboard of the bed and looks eagerly at you. The bird begins to talk! The child is confused and looks thoughtfully at it. He or she asks it if it was actually talking and this was not a dream. The bird too looks surprised as it realizes that the child could understand everything it said. Both of them start talking and soon become good friends! The rare bird grants the child a priceless boon! He or she asks the bird to give him or her mighty wings to fly! The bird willingly grants this earnest wish!

132 Being a Brilliant Thinker

Tickle the Thoughts:

1. Ask the child if the rare bird was talking to him or her.
2. Ask your child what he or she would do with mighty wings.
3. What are the places he or she would visit?
4. Encourage the children to design wings using recyclable material and apply their extensive knowledge to test if it works!
5. Ask the child how he or she can fly.

Goals Achieved
- Better synthesizing and reformulating abilities
- Improved application and testing abilities
- Enhanced analysis and evaluating abilities
- Better ability to seek evidence and draw inference
- Improved understanding and problem-solving abilities
- Better abstract thinking
- Improved creative thinking
- Enhanced analytical thinking
- Better critical thinking

Tick-tack Tips

1. The Wright Brothers, Orville and Wilbur, were undoubtedly the first two American aviation pioneers generally credited with not just inventing but also flying the world's first successful flying plane. The brothers made their first controlled and sustained flight on 17 December 1903, four miles south of Kitty Hawk, North Carolina.

2. Over time, in 1904–05, the brothers developed their flying machine into the first practical fixed-wing aircraft.
3. An interesting fact about these brothers is that both of them never attended college.

Activity–45
Granddad's Birthday!

Proposed Situation:

It is your father's seventy-fifth birthday today and you are planning a surprise party. You want to prepare delicious food, and your husband is supposed to invite your father's friends for the party and do some last minute shopping. Both of you have a lot of work to do before the party begins. Your child, being a responsible member of the family, has been asked to take his or her granddad out of the house for two hours so, you can prepare for the party. Your child, too, wants the party to be a big success, so he or she willingly accepts the responsibility. You have requested your child to keep the secret!

Tickle the Thoughts:

1. Ask the child how they will keep the secret from his or her granddad.
2. Ask the child how he or she will take granddad out of the house for two hours.
3. Ask them why they have been given such a big responsibility.

Activity–45

🎯 Goals Achieved:
- Better concrete thinking
- Improved convergent thinking
- Enhanced creative thinking
- Better analytical thinking
- Enhanced sequential (linear) thinking

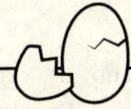

Tick-tack Tip
When parents express faith in the child's unique capabilities, they become responsible for their actions. Share responsibilities with the children whenever possible. Encourage and compliment them genuinely whenever possible.

Activity–46

Tinkle in the Toilet!

Proposed Situation:

Your children have had a long day at school and are eagerly waiting for it to get over. Finally, the school bell rings. They board their bus find a comfortable seat to accommodate themselves and they are on their way home. Suddenly, your child feels the need to go to the toilet!

Tickle the Thoughts:

- Ask the children what are public toilets.
- Is is safe to get off the bus and go to the toilet?
- Is it right to take a tinkle on the roadside? Why?

Goals Achieved

- Improved analytical thinking
- Better sequential (linear) thinking
- Enhanced critical thinking

Activity—46

Tick-tack Tips

1. Introduce children to the safety rules they must follow while using the washrooms:
   - Encourage the children to use the cleanest stall.
   - Do not put your personal belongings on the washroom's filthy floor. Hang them instead!
   - Use toilet paper to press the flush button.
   - Wash your hands with warm water.
   - Dry your hands with clean paper towels.
   - Use the paper towel to open the door knobs.

2. Also, share information about the 'Swachh Bharat Abhiyan' with them. It is a nation-wide campaign in India that aims to clean up the streets, roads and infrastructure of India's cities, towns and rural areas. Prime Minister Narendra Modi officially launched the 'Swachh Bharat Abhiyan' campaign on 2 October 2014 in New Delhi. It is India's largest cleanliness drive to date. The mission of the 'Swachh Bharat Abhiyan' aims to achieve an 'open-defecation free' (ODF) India by 2 October 2019, the 150th birth anniversary of Mahatma Gandhi.

Activity–47

Trip in the Hot-Air-Balloon!

Proposed Situation:

It is a long weekend, and you have arranged a 'Hot-Air-Balloon' ride for your family. It is a breezy day, and your children are going to travel in the hot-air balloon for the first time!

You reach the destination, which is at a mountaintop, and your children are waiting for their turn! The ground crew escorts them to their flight. The pilot tells them about his experiences and that he feels like a mighty eagle to see kilometres of breathtaking-scenes. The basket is ready for your children, and they are ready to take off!

Tickle the Thoughts:

1. Ask your child why is it called a 'hot' air balloon.
2. Ask them what should they expect to see.
3. Ask them what are the safety measures taken by the crew.
4,. How does the hot air balloon go up in the sky?
5. Ask your children at what height do they think they will travel in the hot air balloon.
6. Can the pilot control the direction of the wind? What does he control? (E.g., height, etc.)
7. Ask them how do they think they will land.

Activity—47 139

🎯 Goals Achieved:
- Better analytical thinking
- Improved sequential (linear) thinking
- Increased critical thinking

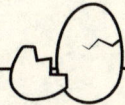

Tick-tack Tips
1. Encourage the children to think about the mechanism of the wind and gravity that helps the balloon take off the ground and land.
2. Encourage them to think and carefully draw the possible experiences they will have during their pleasant journey.

Activity—48

Visit to the Doctor!

Proposed Situation:

Your elder child adores his or her baby sister who has been crying bitterly throughout the night. Your child notices that you and your husband are terribly tired. He or she realizes that he has a crucial match the following morning. However, your child voluntarily joins you for the visit to the paediatrician's clinic to help babysit his little sister.

Tickle the Thoughts:

1. Ask your elder child to check if his or her sister is anxious or worried about going to the doctor.
2. Ask your child if he or she could find a way to calm her down.
3. Ask your elder child what caused the illness.

Goals Achieved
- Strengthened concrete thinking
- Improved analytical thinking
- Better sequential (linear) thinking
- Enhanced critical thinking

Activity-48

Tick-tack-Tip:
Taking the other child along to the doctor's clinic will also help him or her deal with his worries too. Ask the child to help the sibling understand that the doctor is only going to help him or her get better.

Activity–49

Mother's Day Party!

Proposed Situation:

It is the month of May, and your children are excited about the upcoming mother's day. Mother's day falls on the second Sunday of the month. Your children want to celebrate the day to honour their mother. They want to make her feel special on this day!

Tickle the Thoughts:

1. Ask them what they wish to convey to their mother on this memorable day.
2. What kind of presents do they believe will make her happy?
3. Should mothers be made to feel important and special only on such a day?

> **Goals Achieved:**
> - Better memory and association techniques
> - Increased ability to synthesize and reformulate information
> - Enhanced convergent thinking
> - Better analytical thinking

Activity—49

Tick-tack Tips

1. Mother's Day and the joyous celebration of motherhood can be traced back to the ancient Greeks and Romans. They joyfully celebrated grand festivals to honour mother goddess Rhea and Cybele. However, the modern example for Mother's Day is the early Christian Festival known as 'Mothering Sunday'.
2. Children can express their feelings by presenting beautiful, colourful flowers to their mothers. For example, pink carnations represent gratitude and love, red carnations symbolize profound admiration for the mother, and snow-white carnations are in the memory of a mother who is no longer alive.
3. Encourage children to celebrate Father's Day and Grandparents' Day as well.

Activity–50

Pet in the Rocket!

Proposed Situation:

You are taking your children for a summer vacation to a lovely place that is close to a picturesque village. In addition, it is a rocket-launching pad! This time, your children want to take their dog with them, instead of leaving him behind at the crèche.

Your children have carefully packed their bag with their dog's belongings too. You are all set to head out to the village. The dog happily trots along to get into the car. Once you have reached the destination, your pet jumps out of the car and begins to run around, swishing his tail and often barking with excitement. You take your children to their rooms, and they tow their bags.

Your child unzips the pet's bag to open the packet of dog food. He or she pours it into the bowl and affectionately calls the dog. The child eagerly waits for him to show up and calls him again. Yet, the dog is nowhere to be seen. The child then goes looking for him outside. Suddenly, there is a loud announcement, 'The three main engines are now in position, ready for the launch.'

The child conveniently ignores the announcement and continues to look for the dog. The child hears another announcement, 'T-minus 6 seconds', and a loud bark! Your child hears the countdown and an announcement, 'T-minus 0 seconds', and the solid rocket booster gets ignited and is ready to launch!

Activity–50

Your child watches the rocket take off and then realizes that his or her dog is in it!

Tickle the Thoughts:
1. Ask the children how the dog got inside the rocket.
2. Ask them what is he going to do in the space.
3. Is he going to come back to earth? In how many days or months will he be back?

Goals Achieved
- Extended divergent thinking
- Better creative thinking
- Improved analytical thinking
- Enhanced critical thinking

Tick-tack Tips
1. Introduce the children to launch pads and help comprehend what each announcement refers to.
2. Inform that many intelligent animals have travelled to outer space. The first ones were the fruit flies. The flies reached 108 km and were instantly recovered alive by a parachute.
3. The first monkey to travel in space was Albert II on 4 June 1949.
4. A stray dog from the streets of Moscow, Laika travelled in the Soviet spacecraft Sputnik 2 that was launched on 3 November 1957.

Activity–51

Diwali *Ke Mithai*!

Proposed Situation:

Diwali is the Indian festival of lights celebrated over two days and your children's holidays have already started. You are visiting your sister with your family and carrying a lot of lovely presents for her. Your children meet their aunt and she has prepared lots of good food for them. When you are about to leave for home, she hands over the most beautifully wrapped basket full of goodies to your children and she wishes them a very happy Diwali. The children are thrilled to get the goody basket but choose to be calm and polite! You say goodbye to your sister. Once you have reached home, the children rush to their room to find out the contents inside the basket!

Tickle the Thoughts:

1. Ask the children what the basket consist of.
2. Ask them why the basket was handed over to them.

Goals Achieved:
- Improved communication and presentation skills
- Better decision making abilities
- Better divergent thinking
- Better creative thinking
- Improved analytical thinking

Tick-tack Tips
1. Diwali is traditionally celebrated by millions of Hindus, Sikhs and Jains across the world. The festival coincides with the Hindu New Year, which celebrates new beginnings and the triumph of good over evil and light over darkness.
2. Encourage the children to enjoy the true spirit of the cultural festivities. Allow them to meet and interact positively with the family members. It will encourage them to strengthen family ties.

Activity–52

Santa's Secret Gift!

Proposed Situation

It is Christmas, and your children are looking forward to Santa climbing down the chimney to celebrate the day with them. Your children have done a splendid job with the preparations to welcome Santa. The decorated Christmas tree is ready with a glittering star, buntings and festoons are all in place, and the rich Christmas cake is ready too! They have decorated the Christmas wreath with a lot of care.

Suddenly, the doorbell rings, and they wonder if Santa has taken a different route to surprise them, and they rush to open the door! However, when they open the door, they do not find anyone outside! They step out and look right and left, and yet no one is to be seen. With long faces, they turn around, walk back into the house, and step on an envelope. They pick it up and see their names written on it. They open it quickly to find a beautiful card!

Tickle the Thoughts:

1. Ask the children who do you think had kept the card there.
2. Ask them if it has the initials of the 'Secret Santa' written on it.
3. Does it grant them their wishes?

Activity–52   149

Goals Achieved:
- Enhanced memory and association techniques
- Enhanced abstract thinking
- Better creative thinking
- Improved analytical thinking
- Enhanced critical thinking

Tick-tack Tip
Is Santa real? Encourage the children to know more information between the legendary story and facts about this fictitious character. Help them weigh the facts against the legend.

Activity–53

Pyjama Party!

Proposed Situation:

Your child's school has decided to organize a pyjama party in the evening. The schoolteachers have asked them to arrange everything for the party. As this is for the first time your children will be hosting the party, the schoolteachers have told them to involve five friends to help them.

Tickle the Thoughts:

- Ask the children why it is called a pyjama party.
- How would they prepare for the party?
- Who is going to read a story to them?

🎯 Goals Achieved:
- Enhanced memory and association techniques
- Enhanced abstract thinking
- Increased divergent thinking
- Better creative thinking
- Improved analytical thinking

Tick-tack Tips
1. Encourage the children to organize the complete party on their own. However, watch over them without letting them know they are being watched.
2. If they choose to consider a theme party, support their ideas but do not interfere.

Activity–54

The Lost House Key!

Proposed Situation

You are going out of town for a day and have handed a bunch of keys to your children. You explicitly mention to your children that they have to take care of the keys, else they will be locked out of the house. You leave for work. In the evening, your children lock the house and go cycling with their friends. They then play football and finally are on their way back home. They park and lock their cycles. When they climb the stairs to the apartment and ring the bell, they realize that you are not home today. The eldest child checks his or her pocket for the keys and the pocket is empty!

Tickle the Thoughts:

1. Ask them to think where they remember having the house keys the last time.
2. Ask them if they know where the spare house keys are kept.
3. Where could they have dropped the keys?
4. How are they going to find it?

Activity—54

Goals Achieved:
- Enhanced memory and association techniques
- Increased ability to synthesize and reformulate information
- Enhanced analysing and evaluating abilities
- Improved understanding and problem-solving abilities
- Strengthened concrete thinking
- Deepened convergent thinking
- Enhanced critical thinking

Tick-tack Tip
Children should be encouraged to be responsible but should also have alternatives for one situation. Before leaving the house, parents must ensure that they designate a reliable place for the child to keep the key so that he or she does not require to keep the keys in their pockets before going to play.

Activity–55

Flying Driverless Car!

Proposed Situation:

It is Monday morning and your children are ready to go to school. They kiss you and their Dad goodbye and leave for their bus stop. While waiting for the bus, their friend informs them that school bus is running late. Your child wants to ask you to drop him or her to school but then remembers that you are unwell. The child begins to think about alternatives and realizes that no one else could take him or her to school. What makes matters worse is that the child does not want to miss the first class, which is English, as it is his or her favourite subject. Suddenly, a beautiful flying car lands in front of you. The door is flung open, but there is no one in the driver's seat!

Tickle the Thoughts:

1. Ask the child where could the driver be.
2. How does a flying car work?
3. Ask your child how he or she would like to design a car that can travel through water. What features would it have?

Goals Achieved
- Improved understanding and problem-solving abilities
- Improved analytical thinking
- Better creative thinking
- Improved analytical thinking
- Enhanced critical thinking

Tick-tack Tips
1. Driverless cars are also known as robot cars, autonomous cars. These cars can sense its environment and work with little or no human supervision.
2. Driverless cars include many sensors to work from its surroundings. These are computer vision, GPS, sensory information to identify appropriate navigation paths, etc.
3. The potential benefits of using driverless cars typically include reduced costs, increased safety, increased mobility and better fuel efficiency.

Goals Achieved

-
-
-
-
-

Understanding and Problem-solving

Activity–56

Fall before the Finish Line!

Proposed Situation:

It is Sport's Day today in your child's school, and they have been practicing tirelessly. Your child is running a race. Now, the time has ultimately arrived when he or she is about to run the final race. You see him or her standing on track #2. You hear the announcement, 'On your marks, get set' and the clap. The race instantly begins, and all the talented players are running towards the finish line. Gradually, your child overtakes the other runners, one after the other. He or she is now the fastest runner in the race and has a significant lead. The whole audience is hoping your child to be the first one to reach the finish line. Your notice that your child turns around to see how far the runner up is; he or she loses balance and falls on the track. Your child lifts his or her head and sees that he or she is just a few metres away from the finish line!

Tickle the Thoughts:

1. Ask the child what he or she should do—should he or she get up and run to the finish line?
2. Ask the child what is more important to him or her—finishing the race or winning and why?

Being a Brilliant Thinker

> **Goals Achieved:**
> - Smartened decision making
> - Stimulates quick thinking skills
> - Improved analytical thinking
> - Enhanced critical thinking
> - Improved understanding and problem-solving abilities

Tick-tack-Tip:
1. 'Great is the art of beginning, but greater is the art of ending.'– Henry Wadsworth Longfellow

    It is important for parents and teachers to instill true sporting spirit into children when they are young. Practice makes a person perfect, but after the fall, pulling yourself together, not giving up and getting to the finish line makes a player a true 'sportsperson.'

    M.S. Dhoni, the great Indian cricket team captain, was run out in his first match against Bangladesh for a duck. He did not give up! Later, he became the captain of the Indian cricket team, and he went on to lift the T-20 Cricket World Cup for India in the year 2007 and further went on to win the ODI World Cup 2011.

Activity–57

Visit to the Museum!

Proposed Situation:

The school is taking the children for an excursion to a National Heritage site, the Forest Research Institute Museum in Dehradun, Uttarakhand. Your children have heard lots of good things about Dehradun from their parents and are very excited about the trip. As they travel to Dehradun, they tell their friends about their experiences to the other museums they visited in the past. They are now at the main entrance of the Forest Research Institute at Dehradun. Once the bus is inside the campus and stops for the kids to de-board, every one slowly gets off the bus. The area is a lush green expanse of land, with a huge beautiful building made of millions of bricks and the Himalayas in its backdrop. What a breathtaking view!

Tickle the Thoughts:

1. Does the museum remind them of anything they might have read in a book or seen in a movie?
2. If they could spend the day inside the jungle, what would they like to do?

Being a Brilliant Thinker

> **Goals Achieved:**
> - Enhanced memory and association techniques
> - Improved analytical thinking
> - Enhanced critical thinking
> - Increased ability to synthesize and reformulate information

Tick-tack Tips

1. Share the information with the children:

    The main building was inaugurated in 1929 by the then Major Freeman Freeman-Thomas, first Marquess of Willingdon. It is now a National Heritage site. The Forest Research Institute Dehradun is among the oldest institutions of its kind and acclaimed all over the world. The building was listed for a time in the Guinness Book of Records, as the largest purely brick structure in the world. The main building is an impressive edifice, marrying Greco-Roman and Colonial styles of architecture. The FRI's building houses a Botanical Museum and there are different kinds of trees from around the world.

    There are six sections in the museum:
    1. Pathology Museum
    2. Social Forestry Museum
    3. Silviculture Museum
    4. Timber Museum
    5. Non-wood Forest Products Museum
    6. Entomology Museum

Activity–58

No Electricity!

Propose Situation:

Your children's holidays have started and they are relaxing. They are enjoying baking cupcakes in the microwave and drinking cold water from the fridge. As they laze around under the fan on the couch and switch on the television, they hear a news flash saying that there is going to be no electricity in your area for the next two days!

Tickle the Thoughts:

1. Ask them what would they plan on doing for the next two days, without electricity.
2. Are electricity and light the same?
3. How do they plan to spend the night without light?

Goals Achieved
- Enhanced analysing and evaluating abilities
- Improved understanding and problem-solving abilities
- Enhanced abstract thinking
- Improved visual thinking
- Better creative thinking
- Improved analytical thinking
- Enhanced critical thinking

164 Being a Brilliant Thinker

Tick-tack Tips

Encourage the children to come up with activities that they can enjoy when there is no electricity. It will be an experience for them to live life for two days in a different way. Make a note of all the activities they mention and encourage them to reduce their screen time.

Activity–59

Meeting a Butterfly Fairy!

Proposed Situation:

One pleasant evening, your children are walking leisurely in the garden. They see a gigantic cocoon shaking in the corner. They slowly go near it to inspect what it is.

All of a sudden, the cocoon begins to crack, and a giant butterfly comes out of it. They children run helter-skelter and hide behind a tree. One of them gathers courage to peep from behind the tree to see what is happening. He or she sees the giant butterfly has beautiful white wings, and she is wearing a glittering crown, but she seems upset and is crying. The child gathers some more courage to go closer to her and finds that one of her wings is stuck under a lofty branch of the tree. The child looks into her eyes and feels the pain she is in. The child walks closer to her and tries to lift the branch. The branch is heavy, and he or she fails to lift it. The child then decides to put in all his or her strength to help her. This time the child pushes the branch with all his or her might and the butterfly quickly removes her wing from under the branch. Ah! Finally, she is relieved of pain and is now smiling. The child, too, feels good. As she spreads her wings, the child notices that she looks more like a human. She is holding a silver wand in her hand! She looks at the child, and smiles to say thank you and grants three wishes!

Being a Brilliant Thinker

Tickle the Thoughts:
1. Where did the enormous cocoon come from?
2. Ask your child to sketch and colour the picture of the giant butterfly fairy.
3. Ask them about the three wishes.

Goals Achieved:
- Enhanced memory and association techniques
- Improved abilities of application and testing
- Enhanced analysing and evaluating abilities
- Improved understanding and problem-solving abilities
- Deeper abstract-visual thinking
- Better creative thinking
- Improved analytical thinking
- Enhanced critical thinking

Tick-tack-Tips:
1. Encourage them to think about every little detail of the scene and then ask them to draw, colour and paint the entire episode in four to five pictures. Encourage them to make a picture story in a logical sequence of the events. Ask them to add as many details as possible.
2. Help them make speech bubbles of their conversation and encourage them to write it too.

Activity–60

Tell a Fairy Tale Day!

Proposed Situation:

You have narrated many fairy tales to your children at bedtime. Now, they narrate these stories to their friends at school. The teacher informs the whole class that the school is celebrating 'Tell a Fairy Tale Day' the coming Friday. She further informs that the students can choose from the countless whimsical fairy tales—from old ones to those from modern times. They can even choose to create their own tale and role-play characters such as elves, fairies, gnomes and more, but the story must be enchanting. Your children instantly choose to participate in this event.

Tickle the Thoughts:

1. Ask the children which fairy tale they will choose.
2. Ask them if they would like to tell their own fairy tale. Who would the characters be? Why?
3. Which character will they choose to role-play?
4. Design the accessories to enhance the character.

Goals Achieved:
- Enhanced memory and association techniques
- Increased ability to synthesize and reformulate information
- Improved abilities of application and testing
- Enhanced analysing and evaluating abilities
- Better able to seek evidence and draw inference
- Improved understanding and problem-solving abilities
- Enhanced abstract thinking
- Extended divergent thinking
- Better creative thinking
- Improved analytical thinking

Tick-tack Tips
1. Great stories offer the creative potential to transform the lives of the readers. Stories enhance their imaginations and direct those incredible things to prepare them for successful futures.
2. Encourage the children to imagine a story and develop the script. Furthermore, memorize the script and deliver the dialogues on the stage.
3. Encourage them to think about every little detail of the scene in their mind and then ask them to draw, colour and paint the entire episode in four to five pictures. Encourage them to make a picture story in a sequence of the events. Propose them to add as many details as possible.
4. Support the children to create their own storybook and not just print it but publish it too!

Activity—61

A Giant Robot Friend!

Proposed Situation:

Your children's holidays have started, and they are all excited to go outdoors and play with your friends. They get dressed, have their evening snack and kiss you goodbye. As they head outdoors, they notice a few unfamiliar faces in the playground. They remember that their friend's cousin was supposed to visit him. Your children walk up to them and say, 'Hello', but to their surprise, they don't respond! They call out to their friend, but he looks away. Their friend's cousin gives them a cold look and tells them not to disturb them or else they will thrash them! The children are upset; they sit at the corner of the junkyard with no one to play with.

Suddenly, they feel the junkyard move. They think it is an earthquake. They are scared and look around for their parents, but nobody seems to be around. The earthquake instantly seems to be shaking the whole earth and getting more and more severe. The children begin to sweat! They hide under the bench and try to see what is happening. They see that the junk is now assembling into a giant robot!

They shut their eyes, but the thumping gets closer and closer to them. Suddenly, the noise stops, and they are tempted to open their eyes. They see the giant robot standing in front of them and has numerous lights flashing in all directions.

It says, 'My name is Robot.'

Being a Brilliant Thinker

Tickle the Thoughts:
1. Ask the children if the robot is a friend or a foe.
2. Ask them about its creator.
3. Ask them if they can create one at home by using recyclable materials.

Goals Achieved
- Better Memory and association abilities
- Improved ability of synthesizing and reformulating-information
- Enhanced analysing and evaluating abilities
- Improved ability to collate evidence and inference
- Better understanding and problem-solving abilities
- Better abstract thinking
- Improved convergent thinking
- Enhanced analytical thinking
- Better critical thinking

Tick-tack Tips
1. Encourage them to think about every little detail of the scene in their mind and then ask them to draw, colour and paint the entire episode in four to five pictures. Encourage them to carefully think of a picture story in a logical sequence. Propose to add as many details as possible.
2. Ask them to make speech bubbles of their pleasant conversations and encourage them to write them too.

Activity–62

A Milkshake with Superman!

Proposed Situation:

You had offered your children milkshake for breakfast, which they had refused because it wasn't tasty enough. In school, your children are now hungry and there is still time for lunch break. They go to the classroom and sit on their chair with their heads on the table. Suddenly, they feel someone sit next to them. They look up and see Superman sitting right next to them! They look at him and notice that he has a big glass of milkshake for them!

Tickle the Thoughts:

1. Ask your children how Superman got there.
2. Ask them how he knows about the milkshake.
3. Ask them what they are going to say to him.

> **Goals Achieved**
> - Better memory and association abilities
> - Improved ability of synthesizing and reformulating ideas
> - Enhanced analysing and evaluating abilities
> - Improved ability to collate evidence and inference
> - Better understanding and problem-solving abilities

172 Being a Brilliant Thinker

- Better abstract thinking
- Improved convergent thinking
- Enhanced analytical thinking
- Better critical thinking

Tick-tack Tips
1. Encourage the children to talk to Superman about any mealtime issues.
2. Ask them to eat food and write a list of food preferences to become as strong and powerful as Superman.

Activity–63

Suitcase on the Road!

Proposed Situation:

Your husband is driving the car, and your child is sitting in the passenger seat. You are sitting behind your husband with your pet dog named Chikoo. All of a sudden, your child yells out,

'Look out, Dad! There's a suitcase on the road.'

Dad steps on the brakes and brings the car to a stop just in time. Your child steps out of the car and walks towards the suitcase.

Tickle the Thoughts:

1. Ask the child if he or she should touch or open the suitcase.
2. Ask him or her what is inside it.
3. How can they find the owner of the suitcase?
4. Should they be keeping it?
5. Ask them if the owner of the suitcase is worried.

Goals Achieved:
- Better memory and association abilities
- Improved ability of synthesizing and reformulating ideas
- Improved ability to collate evidence and inference

- Better understanding and problem-solving abilities
- Better critical thinking
- Improved convergent thinking
- Enhanced analytical thinking
- Better concrete thinking

Tick-tack Tips
1. Ask the children to think carefully before they even go close to an unidentified object such as a suitcase lying on the road.
2. Encourage them to inform the police to investigate it further before they touch it.

Activity–64

When Sam Ran Away!

Propose Situation:

Sam, a dear friend of your children, was upset once again. In fact, it appeared that he always got upset with petty things. Whenever he did not have his way, he would behave in an unpleasant manner. If anyone corrected him, he would snarl at the person. Whenever he was upset, he would threaten people to run away from home. Although he was only seven years old, he thought himself to be much older.

One day, his Mom was unwell, and Dad requested him to get a few things from his aunt next door. It was when Sam was about to play with your children; Sam got upset again. Instead of going to his aunt's home, he walked out of his home!

Tickle the Thoughts:

1. Ask your children where Sam has gone.
2. Ask them if Sam's behaviour of getting upset with petty things is appropriate.
3. Ask them what kind of behavior is expected of Sam.
4. Ask them if they think Sam was safe after leaving home.
5. Ask them ways to find Sam and talk to him about coming back home.

Being a Brilliant Thinker

Goals Achieved
- Better application and testing abilities
- Improved analysis and evaluation techniques
- Better understanding and problem-solving abilities
- Better critical thinking
- Improved convergent thinking
- Enhanced analytical thinking

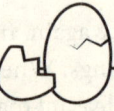

Tick-tack Tips
1. Encourage the children to think critically.
2. While proposing the situation to the children, do not employ your child's name in place of Sam. However, emphasize on the solutions provided by the child and facilitate their thinking in the right direction.

Activity—65

Feeding the Animals!*

Proposed Situation:

Your children are walking cautiously on the local road and see a kitten mewing on the roadside. She appears to be upset, and they don't see the Momma cat anywhere around. Many people on the road are walking past the kitten, but no one seems to be bothered about the traumatic little being. Your children find a secure place at the corner of the street to observe the adorable kitten. They have waited for a long time and are now getting impatient!

Tickle the Thoughts:

1. Ask the children what makes them think that the kitten is crying.
2. Ask them how they can help the kitten.
3. Ask them what safety measures they need to take before going close to the kitten.
4. Ask them how they can make people more sensitive towards street animals.

---

*Story Credit: Kuber Sehgal

Goals Achieved
- Better memory and association abilities
- Improved ability of synthesizing and reformulating ideas
- Better application and testing abilities
- Improved ability to collate evidence and inference
- Better understanding and problem-solving abilities
- Better critical thinking
- Improved convergent thinking
- Enhanced analytical thinking
- Better concrete thinking

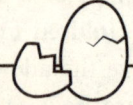

Tick-tack Tip

Unless the child has a pet allergy, it is good to keep animals close to children. Children learn to be responsible and empathetic towards them. They experience lessons that books can barely teach.

Activity–66

The Mango Tree!*

Proposed Situation:

Mango is the king of fruits, and your children are enjoying eating them. In your garden, your children would pick as many mangoes as their hands and pockets could carry.

You, too, are fond of mangoes and so is your husband, who likes to walk up and down the garden relishing the smell of different kinds of mangoes.

One day, your children set out to the garden for a stroll, hoping that they would have a fat, succulent mango or two. However, when they reach the mango tree, they see that it is bare. There was not one mango on the tree. Even the very big one, which Dad had been watching with such pride and anticipation, had disappeared!

Tickle the Thoughts:

1. Ask your children if a powerful wind had blown all the mangoes away.
2. Ask them who could have taken all the mangoes.

---

*Story Credit: Kuber Sehgal

180 Being a Brilliant Thinker

Goals Achieved
- Better memory and association abilities
- Improved ability of synthesizing and reformulating ideas
- Better application and testing abilities
- Enhanced analysing and testing abilities
- Improved ability to collate evidence and inference
- Better understanding and problem-solving abilities
- Better critical thinking
- Improved convergent thinking
- Enhanced analytical thinking

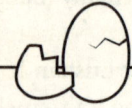

Tick-tack Tips
1. Encourage the children to come up with ideas as to what could have happened and how they can take care of mangoes in the next season!
2. Encourage them to carefully make a fence and a scarecrow to guard the mango tree.

Activity—67

Thirsty Summer!

Proposed Situation:

Your children's summer vacations have started and they are all ready to play throughout the day with their friends. You have asked them to carry a bottle of water to keep them hydrated all the time. However, in a hurry, they forget to carry their bottles and leave when their friends call out for them.

It is half past eight in the morning and the children are enjoying the football match. The game continues for a while, and they notice that their friends' parents are asking them to break for lunch.

Your children then realize that it is two o'clock! Your children sit on the bench talking to their friends and then bid them goodbye.

As soon as one of them gets up from the bench, he feels everything around him is spinning. He looks at the bench and sees it is spinning, too. He hears a loud and shrill noise in his ears!

Tickle the Thoughts:

1. Ask the children what is happening to him.
2. Ask them what they should do to avoid this feeling the next time.
3. Ask them why is water essential for the body.

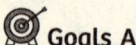 Being a Brilliant Thinker

🎯 Goals Achieved
- Better memory and association abilities
- Better application and testing abilities
- Enhanced analysing and evaluating abilities
- Better understanding and problem-solving abilities
- Better critical thinking
- Improved concrete thinking
- Improved convergent thinking
- Enhanced analytical thinking

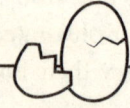

Tick-tack Tips
1. Ask the children to drink enough water during the summers.
2. As you propose the situation to the children, encourage them to eat healthy and nutritious food. Help them come up with a food menu each month such that they get a balanced diet.

Activity–68

Terry's Medicine!

Proposed Situation:

Your children's best friend is their next-door neighbour Terry. Terry is not feeling well today. She seems frail and pale. Her mother calls the doctor and he diagnoses her with a viral fever. He says, 'She has the viral fever and will be well soon, but Terry should have the medicines on time.' She needs to have the medicines every six hours.

Your children visit Terry after a few days, but they are surprised to see her still unwell. Her mother gives Terry the medicine and starts talking to your children. While they are still talking to her mother, they notice Terry throwing the medicines into the dustbin next to her bed!

Tickle the Thoughts:

1. Ask the children why Terry is still unwell.
2. Ask them if they should tell Terry's mother about their findings.

Being a Brilliant Thinker

Goals Achieved
- Better analyzing and evaluation abilities
- Improved ability to collate evidence and inference
- Better understanding and problem-solving abilities
- Enhanced concrete thinking
- Better critical thinking
- Improved convergent thinking
- Enhanced analytical thinking
- Better sequential (linear) thinking

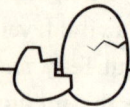

Tick-tack Tip
Encourage the children to come up with answers. Ask them if it is important to side by their friend in doing something that can harm him or her. Help them understand it is nice to love your friends, but when they are doing something wrong, as good friends, it is their responsibility to check them.

Activity–69

One Stormy Evening...!

Proposed Situation:

Mahi was an unhappy boy. He is also your child's best friend. He was visiting the seaside for a vacation. He took a bucket and a spade to play on the beach after dinner.

Even though he had had his favourites for dinner, he was still unhappy. He was cross and wore an ugly scowl on his face. Mahi's father looked at him and noticed his pout. He tried to cheer up the boy.

He said, 'Mahi, come and help me build a castle.'

Trying to make things easy for his son, he added, 'The tide will rise soon, and we will be able to watch it come close to the sand castle!'

Mahi replied, 'I don't want to build any castle.'

'Come on,' his Dad tried to encourage him, 'I know you like building castles.' But Mahi walked away.

'Alright,' said his Dad, 'I will build it all by myself.'

Mahi trudged along the beach farther and farther away from his Dad. He just wanted to be left alone, away from friends and family. He had lost track of time.

Suddenly, he heard a loud thunder and looked up. He could no longer see the deep blue sky. A dark blanket of cloud was looking down at him. He heard another thunder and saw the lightening crack through the sky.

186 Being a Brilliant Thinker

Mahi got scared. He looked around but found nobody on the beach!

Tickle the Thoughts:

1. Ask your children how Mahi is supposed to behave.
2. Ask them if they can conclude the story.

> ### 🎯 Goals Achieved
> - Better analyzing and evaluation abilities
> - Enhanced concrete thinking
> - Better critical thinking
> - Improved convergent thinking
> - Enhanced analytical thinking

> ### Tick-tack Tip
> Encourage the children to conclude the proposed situation on an optimistic note. Ask them to propose the 'good behaviour' guidelines and practise solutions to manage naughty temperament. Encourage them to find calming practices that work for them in an odd situation.

Activity–70

The Treasure Chest!

Proposed Situation:

One day, your children decide to learn the advance level of deep sea diving with their parents. They have never done it before, but you and your husband decide to take them for a crash course. They learn the techniques fast and soon are prepared for the final day.

They are ready to dive. As all of you are swimming deeper and deeper into the water, you see a treasure chest at the bed of the ocean!

Tickle the Thoughts:

1. Ask the children how the water felt.
2. Ask them what all they saw around them.
3. Ask them what they think the treasure chest contains.

Goals Achieved

- Better analysing and evaluation abilities
- Enhanced concrete thinking
- Better critical thinking
- Improved convergent thinking
- Enhanced analytical thinking

Being a Brilliant Thinker

Tick-tack Tips
1. Encourage the children to think about the specific details of the unique situation as far as possible.
2. Help them explain the features of the treasure chest. Then, ask them to draw or paint it.

Activity–71

Grandpa's Radio!

Proposed Situation:

Your children are visiting their grandparents for their holidays. They notice a nice big box lying in the corner of the big house and ask their grandfather about the box.

Their grandfather tells them it is a radio! This was the first time your children are seeing a radio. They request their grandfather to switch on the radio. He asks your children to assist him move the radio from the corner of the house and place it on a table that is next to the socket. He plugs it into the wall socket. Your children are excited to hear the music, and they begin to turn various knobs on the radio set.

All they could hear were grunts, squeaks and roars but no music.

The children try to turn the knobs this way and that, turn the current on and off, but whatever they tried failed!

They run to their grandfather for help. He turns a few knobs, pushes buttons and hears the radio squeak. He looks at the children over his spectacles and smiles at them. He tells them, 'We shall call for skilled hands to check the radio.' The grandfather calls his friend, who knows how to fix radios and asks him to come over at once.

The next day, his friend comes over and begins to work. He works for a while with his head buried into the set, and then he

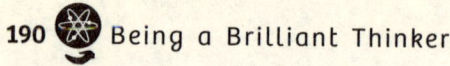 Being a Brilliant Thinker

pulls himself together and says, 'Let us try plugging it in now.'

Tickle the Thoughts:

1. Ask the children what they expected to hear the first time the radio was plugged in.
2. Ask them if their grandfather's friend was skilled. How can they judge him?
3. Ask them what happened after the friend plugged the radio into the wall socket.

Goals Achieved
- Enhanced memorizing and association techniques
- Improved synthesizing and reformulating abilities
- Better analyzing and evaluation abilities
- Improved ability to collate evidence and inference
- Better understanding and problem-solving abilities
- Enhanced concrete thinking
- Better critical thinking
- Improved convergent thinking
- Enhanced analytical thinking
- Better sequential (linear) thinking

Tick-tack Tips
1. Encourage the children to think about all the details of the situation. Ask 'what if' questions to further encourage them to find solutions.
2. Help them explain to you various ways to repair a radio.

Activity–72

Crown in the Garden!

Proposed Situation:

Your children are walking in the lush green expanse of the garden in their aunt's picturesque village. They look up at the exuberant clusters of flame-red flowers blooming on the Gulmohar trees. They hear birds chirping on its branches. The mountains lie in the distance shaped like a camel's hump, or like that of the nose of a slumbering giant. As they walk ahead, they step on something pointed. They look at the ground to find a beautiful crown covered with mud and dry grass. They hear the tinkering of bells when they pick it up to dust off the mud.

They notice that the mud has turned into pixie dust and is floating in the air!

Tickle the Thoughts:

1. Ask the children what will happen next.
2. If they place the crown on their heads, will they be granted boons? What will they grant people who are yet to learn to be good?
3. Ask them the best way to help people recognize the difference between good and bad.

Being a Brilliant Thinker

> ### Goals Achieved
> - Better analyzing and evaluation abilities
> - Enhanced application and testing abilities
> - Enhanced divergent thinking
> - Better critical thinking
> - Enhanced analytical thinking
> - Better creative thinking

Tick-tack Tip

When children mentor others to realize the difference between good and bad, they first have to internalize the morals in the situations.

Activity–73

Invisible Me!

Proposed Situation:

Your children's school is taking them to a chemistry laboratory to watch how experiments are performed. They are excited about their first visit. The students in their class are queued up, and they are heading towards the laboratory. They are now standing in front of the chemistry teacher, who is showing them various equipment and chemicals.

One of the children is pushed by the students but manages to balance himself. However, he knocks off a few bottles from the shelf next to him. The colourful liquids fall on his clothes, but he quickly takes his position to listen to the teacher.

Suddenly, he hears the teacher call out his name. He walks up to the teacher and stands next to her. She once again announces his name. He looks at her and continues to stand next to her. One of his friends says, 'He must have gone to the washroom, Ma'am!' She continues teaching the class. The bell rings and the students are again queued up and to do back to the classroom.

The bell rings for the lunch break, and your child notices that none of his friends are talking to him. He begins to feel more and more uncomfortable, but chooses to ignore them and goes to the washroom. As he enters the washroom, the children inside start screaming, 'Ghost, ghost!' and run away. However, he decides not to engage in this game!

When he crosses the mirror, he notices that he can't see himself in it. He moves left and right, and front and back, but still is unable to see himself in the mirror.

Tickle the Thoughts:
1. Ask your children what has happened to him.
2. Ask them why could he not see the reflection on the mirror.
3. Ask them what could the mixing of correct chemicals do.
4. Ask them would they like to be visible again.
5. Ask them to share their experiences as an invisible person.
6. Ask them how they can support a good cause by being visible or invisible.

> **Goals Achieved**
> - Improved synthesizing and reformulating abilities
> - Enhanced application and testing abilities
> - Better analyzing and evaluation abilities
> - Improved ability to collate evidence and inference
> - Better understanding and problem-solving abilities
> - Enhanced concrete thinking
> - Better critical thinking
> - Improved convergent and divergent thinking
> - Enhanced analytical thinking
> - Better sequential (linear) thinking
> - Improved creative thinking

Activity–73

Tick-tack Tip

'With great power, comes great responsibility.'– Spiderman
Encourage the children to believe that when they become invisible, they will need to take the responsibility to help the world achieve greater and more meaningful heights. Help the people heal and work towards one objective that will make a better world.

Activity–74

The Security Guard!

Proposed Situation:

Your child's class teacher is organizing a role-play session for all the students the next week. It is compulsory for every child to participate in this event. The teacher decides to make small chits for each child to pull out from a bag. The child will have to role-play the name of the person written on the chit.

The bag full of chits is ready, and all the children are pulling out their chits. Your child's name has been called out, and he is walking towards the teacher. He slips his hand into the bag and hears the soft crumpling of paper. He, finally, pulls out a chit and reads it aloud, 'The Security Guard'. He feels de-motivated, as the wished to play the role of a teacher. He goes back to his seat and waits for the school to get over. The bell rings, and everybody rushes back home. Your child packs his bag and heads towards the school bus. As he passes the school's gate, he catches a glimpse of the school's security guard. He is wearing big dark sunglasses. He remembers that the guard unlocks the gate for the students everyday but never smiles. However, when he looks at your child that day and smiles at him.

The next day, when you go to drop your child off to the school, the security guard stops you at the gate. He tells you something and hands over a pass to enter the school. Somehow, your child gets upset to see that you were stopped at the gate and had to wait with him in the sun. He asks you why the security guard had stopped you at the gate. You explain to him, 'It is extremely important for him to give every visitor a pass and take down the details of the visitor.'

You further explain that the security guard of the school are the most responsible people and look after the safety and security of the children. You also tell him about their long working hours. Lastly, you add, 'I have a very responsible security guard at my office!'

Tickle the Thoughts:

1. Ask your child if he or she would like to role-play the 'Security Guard' and why.
2. Ask him or her about the roles they would want to enact.
3. Ask them what a security guard protects while they are asleep at home.

> **Goals Achieved**
> - Enhanced memorizing and association techniques
> - Improved synthesizing and reformulating abilities
> - Enhanced concrete thinking
> - Better critical thinking
> - Improved convergent thinking
> - Enhanced analytical thinking

Tick-tack Tip
It is important for children to learn to respect all kinds of jobs. Help them rise above the differences based on designation and status of a person.

Activity–75

The Secret Door!

Proposed Situation:

Your children are going on a holiday to an organic farm and are excited to live in a picturesque cottage for three nights with you! Your husband tells them that the cottage is extremely nice and offers various facilities to make their stay enjoyable. The children wake up early and prepare for the trip. Your husband carefully verifies the visit and checks the route to the farm. You have packed a yummy breakfast for them. Now, all of you are on your way to the farm. The pastures on both sides of the road keep you and the children charmed.

The cottage is situated away from the hustle-bustle of the city. Your children help you check into the cottage. They take a tour of the place. It is a beautifully built cottage and has one room on the ground floor and another room on the first floor. Your children go upstairs and decide to sleep in one of the rooms.

They are served dinner and are told to change into their night clothes. They get their favourite storybook and begin to read.

Suddenly, they hear someone whisper their names. They look around to check if their parents are around. But no! Nobody is around. They think to themselves, 'Seems like we are too involved in reading the storybook,' and they continue reading till they hear their names again. This time the whisper was loud and clear. They decide to look for their parents downstairs and find out if they are calling them. But their parents are fast asleep.

On their way back to the room, they find a small door in the staircase. They hesitantly walk towards it and hear the voice again. By now, the children are a bit scared. They reach out to the small wooden knob with their trembling hands and feel the sweat trickle down their foreheads. To their surprise, the knob turns on its own, and the door is left ajar!

Tickle the Thoughts:
1. Ask the children who is behind the door.
2. Ask them where the door leads.
3. Ask them if they should venture out without informing their parents.

Goals Achieved
- Enhanced application and testing abilities
- Better analyzing and evaluation abilities
- Improved ability to collate evidence and inference
- Better understanding and problem-solving abilities
- Enhanced concrete thinking
- Better critical thinking
- Enhanced abstract thinking
- Improved convergent and divergent thinking
- Enhanced analytical thinking
- Better sequential (linear) thinking
- Improved creative thinking

Tick-tack Tip

Encourage the children to complete the story. Allow them to come up with what they believe is behind the concealed door. It may assist parents to understand the deep fears of the child and offer the parents the opportunity to facilitate their thinking in the appropriate direction.

Conclusion

In traditional schools where teaching takes place at the comparable level of factual knowledge only, the academic focus primarily remains on convergent thinking. Children are committed to respond with conventionally standardized answers rather than exploring creative solutions.

Thinking is not accidental. The effort of parents and facilitators and their awareness and hard work together help to enhance creativity in children. They help develop the capacity of the child to think effectively, contribute and continue to upgrade and evolve their thinking skills.

Effective education will empower the emerging generations to be successful. This is undoubtedly the futuristic approach towards deeper learning that children need today. Motivated and independent thinking in the child empowers him or her to diligently pursue their love for learning and achieve goals.

Conclusion

Acknowledgements

I thank my immediate family for helping and supporting me, while I immersed myself in writing this book.

Writing a book is harder than I thought it would be, but, at the same time, it is more rewarding than I ever imagined. None of this would have been possible without my friends. I thank them for providing a constant source of strength.

I am forever indebted to Ms Yamini Chowdhury for her editorial help, keen insights and ongoing support in thoughtfully bringing my ultimate dreams to life.

My sincere thanks to Saswati Bora for willingly giving her inputs, Anurupa Sen for editing this book, Raj Kumari for typesetting and Amrita Chakravorty for intelligently designing the attractive cover of this book. I thank everybody at Rupa Publications for investing their time and collaborative effort in shaping the book to its present form.

To gratefully acknowledge is to admirably express my sincere gratitude to all of you who have been an integral part of this extraordinary journey.

It is for you that this book has become a reality.

Notes

Notes

Notes

Notes

Notes